His Will, Not Mine

GINA MOORE

His Will, Not Mine
Trilogy Christian Publishers A Wholly Owned Subsidiary of Trinity Broadcasting Network
2442 Michelle Drive Tustin, CA 92780
Copyright © 2023 by Gina Moore
All scripture quotations are taken from the Holy Bible, New International Version®, NIV®. Copyright © 1973, 1978, 1984, 2011 by Biblica, Inc.TM Used by permission of Zondervan. All rights reserved worldwide. www.zondervan.com. The "NIV" and "New International Version" are trademarks registered in the United States Patent and Trademark Office by Biblica, Inc.TM.
No part of this book may be reproduced, stored in a retrieval system, or transmitted by any means without written permission from the author. All rights reserved. Printed in the USA.
Rights Department, 2442 Michelle Drive, Tustin, CA 92780.
Trilogy Christian Publishing/TBN and colophon are trademarks of Trinity Broadcasting Network.
Cover design by: Kelly Stewart
For information about special discounts for bulk purchases, please contact Trilogy Christian Publishing.
Trilogy Disclaimer: The views and content expressed in this book are those of the author and may not necessarily reflect the views and doctrine of Trilogy Christian Publishing or the Trinity Broadcasting Network.
Manufactured in the United States of America
10 9 8 7 6 5 4 3 2 1
Library of Congress Cataloging-in-Publication Data is available.
ISBN: 979-8-88738-737-6
E-ISBN: 979-8-88738-738-3

PREFACE

As I sit here in the emergency room, gasping for every breath, I think, *This COVID-19 is real.* I literally cannot get air in my lungs. I wish I could just pass out. Why am I not passing out? This is so bad. Jesus, where are You? Is this how my life is going to end? Why am I so afraid? I am so scared of dying. Why? I believe in Jesus, and I believe in heaven. Why am I so afraid?

FOREWORD

My prayer is for all of those that read this book. Lord, please give them clarity as they read, and allow them to see past me and my experiences and incorporate Your will, direction, and discernment into all of their circumstances. I pray that You would use me as an instrument to speak to the hearts of those that You have purposed. I now remove myself and ask that the Holy Spirit take over. In Jesus' name, I pray. Amen.

As the Lord directs me in writing this book, He will use me to express the lessons that I have learned through tragedies and failures. Know that the Lord has led me to write this book, and the purpose is in no way to highlight the tragedies I have encountered to be the focus of this book. We will all suffer in this life (John 16:33), and most of us will experience at least one tragedy, if not more. This book is solely being written to explain the relevant spiritual lessons that I have learned in hopes that it will help someone else understand how the Lord can turn around tragedies and allow them to be used for His glory and for our spiritual growth. The Lord has shown me, through these tragedies, some truths that I believe we all have either been misinformed about or just purely misunderstood. I pray that the revelation that you will receive while reading this book will allow you to live through the good and bad with peace.

In this book, I will allow the Lord to direct me. I am not responsible for the success of this book. If it gets into one person's hands, the person God needs to read it, then it is a huge success, and to God and my Lord, Jesus Christ, be the glory. Maybe God's intentions are not for this book to be printed and become successful, as the world measures success. Maybe He just wants to know that I will follow His will when I know what it is. Maybe I am the only one who will read this. Whatever it is, it's for Him. I feel like Peter walking out on the water, but I know that Jesus is calling me to do this, so I must keep moving forward, knowing that He is responsible for it all.

TABLE OF CONTENTS

Our Face to the World 1
When the Lord Directs 3
God's Glory, Not Ours 5
From the Beginning.........................9
The Day When Wisdom Was Revealed............21
Our Past..................................37
This Place Is Not Our Home..................49
Getting Angry with God 53
The Lord's Will?..........................57
Spiritual Amnesia 59
The Journey Is Long.......................63
And Then Came the Pandemic.................67
Jesus Is Coming Back, Whether We Believe It or Not ..79
Knowing God versus Knowing of God............85
Feelings and Faith........................97
Hearing from God 103
His Peace Blows My Mind 107
Life Is Hard 111
Falling in Love with Jesus....................119
The Lord Needs Warriors, Not Whiners...........127
The Final Chapter 131
About the Author.........................137

OUR FACE TO THE WORLD

No matter how well we polish up and hide behind our smiles, we all have hurts, tragedies, and hollow places that the world nor our closest confidants can see. Trust me, the Lord sees them all, and He is waiting for you to come to Him to allow Him into those places, so He can heal them and replace them with His joy and peace. I know it sounds like a cliché. We have all heard it before. Well, I have lived it, and I have learned some very tangible principles that we have not been taught in many churches. Have I learned anything that will erase the suffering here on this earth? Absolutely not, but I have learned how to take the Lord with me through the suffering to make it better and to allow a purpose for the suffering and have some good come out of it. I am going to share some spiritual truths that may not be popular, and some may be difficult to embrace, but if you will open your heart and allow the Lord to speak to you, I believe you will see that there is a more peaceful way to go through this life until we get to our final destination: heaven.

WHEN THE LORD DIRECTS

Today is October 14, 2019, and the Lord has been directing me to write this book for several years now. I have started it a couple of times, but then I start thinking, *Why would God choose me to write a book? Who would read this book? Why would anyone want to hear my story?* And finally, *I don't think that I can write a book.* What do all these doubts have in common? "I" and "me." Every doubt is focused on me, my talents, and my abilities. I have learned that God *never* asks us to do anything in our own strength or for our own glory. I also believe that He very rarely, if ever, gives us the entire layout or plan. He expects us to walk in faith, knowing that He will lead and direct us at every turning point. I guess the real question is: how do we get to this place of true faith? I mean, all Christians say that they are walking in faith. We get up every morning, most thank God for the day, pray for our children, pray for protection, and so on. It almost becomes a ritual like when we say, "God bless you."

How do we know if we truly have faith? We cannot know until it is tested. God is so smart and knows each one of us so intimately that we are not all tested in the same way. See, God knows how much we can bear and what it will take to bring each of us to a place of true faith. I would dare to say that when we are tested initially, we may panic, and we may fail in our faith because we believe that a true tragedy would not be allowed by a loving father, and if it were allowed, we typically don't know how to react. I think most of us Christians go through our lives believing that some things will never happen to us. Many of us are even taught this in church and by our spiritual leaders. We are taught that a loving God will protect us from all evil in this world. If we believe tragedy could happen to us, we somehow put it out of our minds and stay nice and tucked away in our Christian bubble.

As I stated, most likely, in this life, we all will endure tragedy, and most will not be spiritually ready. If we are strong, which I would like to think that I am, we can deal with most of what life throws at us. We deal with day-to-day inconveniences in our own strength, but what happens when that tragedy comes along that knocks you totally off of your emotional, physical, and, most importantly, spiritual balance? What happens when we wake up one day, and our entire life and beliefs are shaken and challenged?

GOD'S GLORY, NOT OURS

Everything God will ever ask us to do is for His glory and His alone. There are many books on the market about Christians, their trials, and their triumphs. I want to share in this book tragedies that led me to understand just how real God is and how I arrived at a place where I had no choice but to surrender all. I couldn't bear or carry the load that I was carrying any longer. I asked the Lord, "What part of my life and my experiences do you want me to write about? Would you like me to write about how I was born to a prostitute who put me up for adoption? Would you like me to write about how I went from foster home to foster home before being adopted by parents, who though they did the best they could, never really gave me love, or should I say gave me the love I needed and desired so much? Would the book be about me trying to find love in all the wrong places? Or would it be about all the failed relationships?

Would it be about all the many mistakes that I made, and sometimes still do, even though I knew and know Christ?" I never felt good enough, and I definitely never felt worthy enough to be used by God. Would it be how I gave birth to two beautiful children and how at my daughter's tender age of fifteen, she was run over by a car and nearly died? Would it be how I was diagnosed with breast cancer or nearly died from COVID-19? Would it be about all the hidden pains that I have never revealed to anyone? Would it be about all the disappointments and regrets? I know what the Bible says about Him using the foolish things of the world to shame the wise (1 Corinthians 1:27), but Lord, this is a stretch. None of that matters when, deep down inside, you don't feel worthy. No, though I will incorporate many of these experiences and more, this book is more about what I have learned. I will go into the lessons that I have learned as I have gone through the trials, mistakes, and tragedies of this life and how when we trust God and truly let go, He will most certainly turn them around for His glory and for the good of those that love Him (Romans 8:28). Yep, that's for sure.

What I have learned about the Lord is that we *cannot* run from Him, and we cannot hide our hearts. That is the most mind-blowing thing I know about God. You can fool the world, even close friends or family, maybe even your spouse, but the Lord knows the most intimate parts of you. So intimate that sometimes you don't even know that those things are there. You may not know why you can't have good relationships, keep a job, get over the loss of a loved one, or forgive those that have hurt you. The list goes on. We carry so much that hardens us, even to God's love. This hurts Him because He never meant it to be this way.

So, Lord, I ask You to direct my mind, body, and soul as I embark on this mission that You have directed me to. Let the words that I write and the truths that I have learned from You fall on the ears that You have ordained. Thank You for using a lowly soul like me. The grace and mercy that You have shown through my life are totally mind-blowing. I am the least worthy but am made worthy because of what Jesus did for me on the cross.

FROM THE BEGINNING

My earliest memories of childhood are probably around seven or eight. I don't remember too much prior to this. I was adopted by parents who were unable to have children. My adoptive mother had tuberculosis when she was twenty-one and had to have a complete hysterectomy. She and my dad were married and decided to adopt children. They adopted my sister, Tina, first, then my brother, Edward, and then finally, me. I was two and a half years old when I was adopted. I had already been through a few foster homes but have no memory of this time. My adoptive mother was always the type to want to put us on display. This is something that I remember from my early years. We always had the nicest clothes and hair done just right and went to the best schools. My parents were not rich, but they did well for themselves. This was all a show.

At home, as we got older, there was a lot of turmoil in the home. My dad was cheating on my mom, and my dad was molesting my sister. I wasn't aware of the later until about two years ago. My sister always had issues, including sex and drugs. I look back now, and so much made sense. My dad was molesting my sister from middle school and beyond. If that wasn't bad enough, my sister told my mother, and my mother did nothing. It still brings tears to my eyes now. My dad has since found the Lord and has asked for forgiveness. I have forgiven him, but I have never seen him in the same light. He is an amazing man of God now, and I believe he is truly sorry for all of his past mistakes. My sister has had a very hard life, and I attribute this to what my dad and mother did to her. Your mother, at the least, should be one of those people that protect you or at least try. We all want to be loved and protected. I believe this is a basic need of a child, and when it is not in place, it allows the enemy to come in and really use this as an opportunity to lay a foundation for many negative things that can potentially direct you into a life of destruction.

Until you allow the Lord in and allow Him to show you that He and He alone won't disappoint you, we will go through life carrying this. Only the Lord can heal those places and replace the voided areas with His love and acceptance.

As I was growing up in our household, you walked on eggshells. I was always afraid of my dad. I think we all were. He was very mean in many ways. He grew up with very strict and disciplinary guidelines and used those same guidelines on us. One thing I always remember is him putting us in scalding hot water at bath time. If we told him it was too hot, he would scream at us to get in the tub or else. He would boil the water on the stove for the bathtub because he felt the water from the faucet wasn't hot enough. We were never allowed to voice our opinions, and we never had discussions. What he said was the Bible, and you better not challenge it. I could tell that my mother didn't really agree with many of the things he did, but she would never challenge him, at least not in front of us. I look back on my childhood as being very painful for many reasons. I know now that most of these things were spiritual, not physical. My parents never told us they loved us. I now know that the saying "Hurt people hurt people" goes even further: "Unloved people don't love."

I was very insecure and never felt good enough. How can you feel you are worth anything when your biological mother gives you away, and then you don't feel loved and secure with your adoptive parents? It can make the strongest person feel unlovable. When someone said something bad about me, I believed it. Not only did I believe it, but I would analyze it and usually agree that it was true. That is when I began to seek love in places that I shouldn't. I tried drugs and men. I know for a fact that people use drugs and indulge in bad sexual behavior because, for that small period of time, they feel loved and accepted. Isn't that what we all want? We want to be looked at as being smart or pretty or just accepted.

Harsh truth is that these avenues of feeling good and being accepted are not real. It is just what the enemy uses to keep a hold on you and continue you on his wheel of destruction. I now believe there is nothing wrong with wanting love and acceptance, but we look for it in the wrong places. I spent years looking for love in all the wrong places. This type of behavior is a trick of the enemy. It is a fake acceptance that the enemy offers to us. It feels good at the moment, but the end state of your heart and mind is worse than when you first sought it out. This acceptance and worthiness can only be found in Christ. Again, I know this sounds like a cliché, but it is very true. Once I had children, I put all my energy into them. For a while, that sustained me. I finally found something/someone who loved me unconditionally. But now they are grown, and I am alone. Yes, my children and I are very close, and they love me dearly, and I love them, but when they left to go to college, I was left with a void. This time, I didn't seek after the worldly things to fulfill it; I sought after God.

I didn't just make this decision on the spot. Through the years, I have had tragedies that have forced me to seek after God. I had no one else. It makes me sad now because I look at all the time that I missed out on the acceptance of Christ. I don't mean He wasn't there for me, but I didn't invite Him into my life. Until we invite Christ in, He can and only will be on the sidelines. He will always be present, yearning for you to call out to Him, to truly invite Him into your life. Once you totally surrender to Him, it is a peace and a life that is unimaginable. Will you still suffer? Yes, but the suffering is different because He is with you, and you have a consciousness of His presence.

You walk through life daily knowing that He always has your back, no matter what. Just that knowledge makes me smile and gives me such peace. It's sad to say that I don't believe most Christians receive this revelation on this earth. Do they still go to heaven? If they have accepted Christ, I believe yes, but they have missed the relationship with Him here on earth, and it is so exciting and fulfilling. More fulfilling than any relationship you can have here on earth. To wake up in the morning and know that He is there. I didn't say feel Him. Sometimes you feel His presence, but even when you don't, you know

He is there (we will speak about this later). It is like no other experience on this earth, and I have had some crazy, what I thought at the moment, euphoric experiences. They cannot and will never compare to a true relationship with Christ and the daily peace it brings.

Once I graduated from high school, I went into the military. The reason I did this is that I did not want to stay home, and my parents never made it an option for us to go to college, so I was on my own. I went into the military for two years, but it wasn't a good fit, so I never reenlisted after two years. I then moved to Maryland, where I got a job and started working in Corporate America. One thing that is apparent in this world is that if you shine up the outside of something, people think it's worth something. Once the shininess wears off, the essence is displayed, and people don't want to deal with the reality.

I was always attractive, dressed well, and was very articulate, even if I didn't believe I was. I feel like I can truly "talk a good game." I think that's why I am in sales (we will talk about that later in the book). I always had popular friends; people always were drawn to me. I always had an amazing boyfriend *until* the shininess wore off. See, people in this world want the shininess; they don't want the essence. They want to believe that the shininess is the essence. People must understand that *only* Christ can love us unconditionally. Our parents are always there for us, or should be, and I love my children dearly. I believe that this is the closest that we can get to true love on this earth, and that's not true perfection. Even when we love at our best, it is flawed. We disappoint people we love all the time, even unintentionally.

When Jesus said, "He will leave the 99 sheep to go find the lost ones" (Luke 15:4), that means He truly loves those that are desolate. What I love about the Lord is that He will use the ugliest, nastiest things in us to draw us to Him and to be used by Him. He first will uncover all our nastiness, insecurities, failures, and frailties just so that He can go in and heal them. At our best, many of us release some things to God, but some things are just too ugly, or we don't know these things are there. God knows they are there, and He still loves us. This love is hard for us to comprehend. When these things are uncovered, it hurts; and it hurts bad. Most of the time, these things are revealed in failed relationships, addictions, lost loved ones, etc. It's when we are at our weakest that the Lord has the best chance of being invited in. It hurts so bad, but I have learned that if we will just release it and give it to God, He will heal us and fix the issues, or at least heal the pain.

How do we do this? How do we release things to the Lord? The first step, I believe, is acknowledging that He exists and that we want to trust Him. You see, I said, "Want to trust Him." We must be real with God. I have prayed for God to show me how to trust Him and how to love Him because I truly didn't know how. I would pray in the a.m. and go out and sin willfully in the p.m. That's not true love for God, and I wanted that. I have asked the Lord to increase my faith. I have boldly told the Lord, "I do not know how to love You or treat people the way You want me to," and the list goes on and on. I can't say that I am all the way there yet. That's why I didn't understand why God wanted to use me to write this book.

There are still things I haven't given to God. There are still times when He tells me to go right, and I go left. I don't understand why. Maybe it's because I know He will still love me anyways, and I want what I want at the time. Maybe it's because I don't want to go through the pain of letting go and giving everything to Him. The pain cannot be overlooked or avoided, and we humans want the "feel good right now" all the time. We don't think about later. If we thought about later, we would see all the signs that are in front of us and know that the end is coming, and we would take heed. I am not here to speak another doom and gloom about the end times. Those that have eyes to see can see. We don't think about later because that would take some change and suffering right now. We don't want to suffer. I know I don't. We never think about how long eternity is. It's *forever* and *ever*.

I have never read once in the Word where God says He wants us to be comfortable. I do not believe that He is concerned about us being comfortable. He wants us to have peace. He tells us this in John 14:27; peace doesn't mean a void of trouble or suffering. I have had everything in my life lined up as I wanted it (i.e., money, relationship, health is good, kids are good, etc.) and not had peace. That is because only Christ can give us this. Yes, we can have happiness, but not true peace. Christ also wants us to fulfill our purpose on this earth (Psalm 57:2), and, most importantly, He wants to be glorified. We do serve a jealous God (Joshua 24:19) who wants top priority in our life. I have found out that He wants priority in our lives because He wants to be glorified, but He also knows that all other gods will lead to destruction, and He loves us so much that He doesn't want us to go through unnecessary pain and struggles.

As I write this book, I am going to touch on several points. One of the chapters that is going to be near and dear to me is going to be "How I Know God Is Real." This will be my favorite because I think this is a question that no one wants to talk about. Maybe it's just that no one can truly articulate why they believe God is real. I went to church growing up and into my thirties, and my parents told me about Jesus, but that is not how I know He's real. In the aforementioned chapter, I will let you know how I know He's real. It's crazy, though, because even though I know He's real, I don't always do His will. What is that? Why is that? I think sometimes humans have a problem with unconditional love. I remember having a conversation with someone and asking them, "Do you think murderers like Ted Bundy and other serial killers can repent and go to heaven?" They said, "Absolutely not." Where do we get that thinking? When Jesus died on the cross, He died for *all* of our sins, not just the ones that we committed. He didn't just die for the sins that we believe are forgivable. If that is the case, who has the correct list of sins?

Many of us are going to be surprised when we get to heaven, and we don't see many that we thought would be there, and many will be there that we didn't think would be there. We don't judge; the Word dictates and judges, and it says, "All are welcome and have access to His grace." We want to think that all our family and friends will go to heaven. We also believe that the very good and giving people go to heaven. I am sorry to tell you that this is not true. I remember speaking to a pastor who said that the hardest part of his pastoral duties was conducting the funeral of someone he knew didn't know or accept Christ. What do you say? Do you say what the family wants to hear to make them feel better here on earth? We cannot fathom one of our children or spouse suffering for eternity in hell. Because of this, we try not to think about it, or we just convince ourselves that all of our loved ones are in heaven and at peace, when truly that is not what the Word says (1 John 5:13). Please don't throw the book at the wall. I told you that there were going to be some difficult truths in this book, even for me. We would rather enjoy the temporary, happy moments here on this earth and not think about eternity. We would rather go to church and say we believe in God but not live for Him or do His will.

    First John 5:13 is just one of many scriptures which tells us that the ones that go to heaven are those that do the Father's will. The Bible says that "those who love Him, do His will" (John 14:21). It does not say we are perfect and we will not fall and make mistakes, but it means we are daily trying to honor and glorify Him. Let us all keep it real now and acknowledge that we know when we are living for Christ or when we say we will just live as we want to. We know when we are struggling with sin versus living in it. I have learned that if I can live in sin, I am not living for Christ, period. If we can commit sins daily that we know are against God's will, we are definitely not living for Christ.

THE DAY WHEN WISDOM WAS REVEALED

Before I begin this chapter, I want to say that I now know that nothing happens "by chance." I hear many people say, "How can God allow this to happen or that to happen?" I have learned from this chapter's experience that "everything works for the good of those that love the Lord" (Romans 8:28).

February 4, 2015, started out as every day does. It was a Wednesday, and the weather was extraordinarily beautiful for this time of the year. It must have been mid to upper sixty degrees outside. I call it sweater weather. I am off on Tuesdays and Wednesdays, and it's nice because after the kids get home from school, we get to hang out. At this time, I had two children. The loves of my life. Paige was fifteen, and my son, Cross, was fourteen. They are only sixteen months apart, and we are extremely close. On this day, Paige had a friend home to work on a DECA project after school. DECA is an international organization that teaches high school students about business. Paige and her friend (we will call her Abby) were working on a business plan that was due the next day. It was a huge undertaking that they had been working on for weeks. My son, Cross, needed some jeans, so we were going to head out to some stores that were about fifteen minutes from where we lived to do some shopping.

Cross and I arrived at the stores, and he decided to go to one store, and I decided to go to another. The moment that I stepped into the store, my phone rang, and it was Paige's friend (not Abby, but another one that had stopped by to hang with Paige and Abby). I said, "Hello," and this friend (we will call her Alice) said, "Ms. Gina, you need to get to the hospital; Paige has been hit by a car." I know it sounds crazy, but I thought she was kidding, so I responded by saying, "Alice, please don't play like that. It's not funny." I then heard her voice start to break, and she said, "I'm not playing. Paige has been hit by a car." Every parent has had a nightmare about getting "the call," and it is never good.

Most people that know me know that I am horrible in crisis situations. I panic, and I can't get my thoughts or actions together. It is a very bad trait to have. At this point, I called my son on the phone, who was in another store, and told him we had to leave ASAP because Paige had been in an accident. Understand that, at this point, I had no details, but I felt in my heart it was serious. I tell you that "mothers' intuition" is spot on. Well, Cross and I met at the car, but by this time, I was a total basket case. I literally didn't know what to do. Cross tried to keep me calm, but it wasn't working.

A lot of what happened between now and the next twenty-four hours was somewhat of a blur, but I will explain what I remember. Our community is a very tight-knit community. Everyone knows everyone. So, I began calling my close friends to let them know what had happened. I hadn't made a move to do anything because I was panicked. I finally got a very dear friend on the phone who offered to come and pick me up to take me to the hospital where they were taking Paige. I still wasn't thinking or grasping what was going on at this point. This was not a good idea because she was probably thirty minutes away, and by this time, it was rush hour traffic, and the hospital they said they were taking her to was probably forty-five minutes plus away from where I was. In hindsight, I probably should have called 911 and had a police escort take me. I definitely was not in a place to be able to drive.

As I am waiting for my dear friend, I am trying to get information on exactly what happened. My husband and mother were home, and the accident took place directly in front of our home. No one was answering their phones. I finally got my eighty-year-old mother to answer, who doesn't hear very well, and she couldn't understand me. I told her to go outside because Paige had been in an accident. She said, "Paige got a new car?" I was so frustrated. My husband, who works nights, was dead to the world, and though neighbors were banging on the doors trying to let him know what was going on, he didn't wake up. Finally, the next-door neighbor kept dialing my husband's phone and woke him up to let him know that he needed to go outside because Paige had been in an accident.

By this time, police, firemen, and an ambulance were on the scene. We have a police officer who lives a few doors down, and I think that's why they arrived so quickly. One of Paige's friends at the scene said they tried to call 911 several times and couldn't get through. Finally, my husband, Darryn, went outside, and there were police and emergency personnel everywhere. Paige was lying on the ground, awake but not moving. The ambulatory personnel told Darryn that they were going to take Paige to Scottish Rite Children's Hospital in Atlanta, Georgia. At this time, Paige was fifteen years old. My husband didn't have shoes on, and they told him they couldn't wait and that he would have to meet them at the hospital. I, personally, would have jumped in the ambulance without shoes, but I guess that's the mother in me.

Finally, Darryn called me. You have to understand that Darryn is the total opposite of me. He is an ex-cop, now a journalist, and he stays calm in emergency situations. While I'm having a breakdown, he's figuring it out calmly. I knew from the tone in Darryn's voice that it was serious. I asked him what had happened, and he said that Paige's friend, who was driving, had run over Paige by accident. Not run over a foot or a leg, but her entire body. We did not know at this moment, but she was crushed from the neck down. The first thing I said to Darryn was, "Please, don't let anything happen to my baby." He responded by saying, "You need to get to the hospital fast." This is not what I wanted to hear. I wanted to hear that it wasn't that bad and that she seemed okay. Something that would comfort me.

Not sure how much time had passed, but my friend arrived, and Cross and I jumped into her truck. We immediately began praying. Remember, it's right in the thick of rush hour. My worst nightmare was that Paige would die before I arrived at the hospital. This is what was at the forefront of my mind. I was rambling to Jesus. Not sure what I said; just rambling. It's funny because the Lord understands our rambling. We don't need articulate verbiage to be understood by our Father. He made us, and He knows us inside and out. He knows us better than we know ourselves, so He knows what we are trying to communicate no matter how we lay it out. My son was trying to comfort me, and my friend who was driving kept apologizing and saying that she was sorry it was taking her so long to get to the hospital. As if it was in her control. I have learned that, as humans, we believe that we can control so much when we really have no control over anything. Not even our next breath. It's difficult to comprehend this as we go about our life with all of our goals and plans.

    We finally arrived at the hospital, and my friend dropped Cross and me off at the Emergency Room entrance while she went and parked. When we arrived at the hospital, the place was packed. I told you we were a tight community. There were people from church, school, the neighborhood, and Paige's previous schools. When I first walked into the room that had been dedicated to Paige's "people," I saw Paige's friend that ran over her. She was there along with her parents. She was a mess. She was crying and obviously in a shocked state. I don't remember much of what was said, but I think I must have spent at least thirty minutes with her before I went to go see Paige. I comforted her. I told her that we all knew that this was an accident and that we didn't blame her. I even told her about stupid mistakes I had made as a kid and that this would all be okay. Understand I was not aware of my daughters' injuries at this time. At this moment, God needed me to love Abby. I have so many friends that were there, even Christians, who couldn't believe that I spent that much time with her and loved her as I did. To be totally honest, I was on adrenaline and was going through the motions. I do believe that when you are in a crisis, what's truly in you comes out. You don't have time to think about what to say or how to act. I genuinely was not mad at her yet.

When people go through tragic situations, there are no rules on how to handle them. I truly believe that what is in you comes out because you have no energy for a filter. As the days and months go on, I will learn some lessons that are worth more than any tragedy could ever teach me, but if you had asked me if I would have wanted to take this journey to learn them, I would have definitely said no. I know, and I am sure you would agree, that the thought of losing a child is mind-blowing, but to walk it, is something that no human should have to endure.

At this point, at least an hour had gone by, though time was not tangible at this point. I still had not been in to see my daughter. To be totally honest, I was afraid to see her. I was afraid of what I would see and how bad she was. My husband finally came to me and said that she was asking for me. I promised myself that I would not breakdown in front of her no matter how bad it was, though I knew it was bad.

When I walked in, Paige was covered up to her neck with blankets. There were doctors everywhere, and Paige was alert. Her face didn't look bad, just a large scrape on the right side of her face. She began to say how sorry she was, and I said, "Don't worry about it." I told her that I loved her. I only stayed a couple of minutes because I felt myself getting ready to fall apart. Sure enough, when I left her room, I fell to the floor. A lot of this is a blur, so I am recapping what I remember. At this point, the doctor asked to see my husband and me in a separate room. I had watched enough movies to know that when a doctor asks you into one of those small, separate rooms, it's not good. I told my husband I didn't want to go, but that wasn't an option. When we went into the room, the doctor began to speak of the injuries that he knew of at the time, and it wasn't good. Paige had six pelvic breaks; two femurs broke in half and a tibia that had popped right out of her leg. These were just the injuries that were identified at this time. The doctor said that it didn't look good. This is all that I can remember from this initial conversation with the doctor.

The next thing I remember is we were in a room with Paige, and they were giving her pain meds and just allowing her to rest. It's ironic because when the doctor asked Paige if she wanted pain meds, she said no. She had just been run over by a car. This is another lesson that I learned about our gentle Father. He shields us. When Paige told the doctor that she wasn't in any pain, the doctor said, "That's not possible." Yep, "For with God nothing shall be impossible" (Luke 1:37, KJV). My husband and I lay by her bedside as she slept. I lay there and thought about how, in one day, my life would be changed forever. When the sun came up, I remembered thinking how no matter what happens, life goes on. No matter what tragedies or hardships we face in this life, the sun keeps rising and setting, and time keeps progressing.

When morning arrived, the doctors came in and said that Paige's injuries were too extensive for her to be treated at the facility we were in. They needed to get her moved to a trauma facility. The main concern was the six pelvic breaks. Unfortunately, at this point, the doctors didn't feel like she was stable enough to be moved. They decided to induce her into a coma and allow her body to rest. They were now awaiting a bed to open at one of the trauma facilities that she needed to go to. My lessons were about to begin on how God works.

Everyone knows that Grady Hospital is the number one trauma facility in Atlanta. This was one of the facilities that they were trying to get a bed in. Unfortunately, Grady said they had no availability. Time was of the essence, so Gwinnett Medical had an opening before Grady did. I was not happy because I wanted the best for my baby, and I believed that Grady was the best. When and if we truly trust God, we must trust Him with all of the details. We can never go by what we feel, see, or even what we think we know. Our trust must be solely in God's wisdom to guide, direct, and open up the correct doors. When we do this, we don't struggle but have peace in the process. This is not an easy place to get to because, as humans, we feel like we are in control. When we are not in control, we panic. Needless to say, I was not at this place at this moment.

Once we arrived at Gwinnett Medical Center, we waited in ICU until they brought Paige into the room. I had not seen her since she had been incubated. When they brought her in, she was swollen and looked lifeless with the tube down her throat. The doctor met with us and said that time would tell if she would make it. He said that they wanted to let her body rest before trying to put her back together again. Yes, my little girl had to be put back together again.

During this time, I went through a rough struggle. I struggled with God. I knew He was there, but I had no peace and didn't know why. I would soon find out why. I thanked God for being there for me. He responded, "I am where I have always been. It is you that has been too busy to spend time or recognize My presence." Wow, that is powerful. It reminded me of the scripture that says, "He's faithful even we are not" (Timothy 2:13). Even when we don't have time for Him, He is there. He is there waiting, longing for us to acknowledge Him, receive love from Him, and commune with Him. At this point, I continued to reach out to the Lord and tell Him to save my daughter. I pleaded with the Lord not to allow Paige to die. I begged and begged and begged, but still *no* peace. This went on for three days. Every day, the doctors would tell us that they didn't know if she would make it. I would ask, "Is she out of the woods?" and the doctors would say, "I'm sorry, but no." I continued to beg God until I was tired. I was tired of telling God what to do and not seeing the manifestation of it. I finally gave up. I now know this was when I surrendered "my" will for "His" will. I said to the Lord, "If You are going to take her from me, please give me the strength to deal with it." I finally said, "Lord, Your will be done."

This was the turning point of this entire tragedy. This was when I released God to perform. Until I released my faith to say, "Whatever happens, God, I trust You," "Whatever You allow is okay," and "I trust You to do what's best, even if it hurts," I had no peace. The Holy Spirit is getting aroused even as I am typing. See, the Lord showed me that we are continually walking in a state of "do my will" instead of "do His will," and until we get to truly desiring "His will," we will never have true peace and see the fulfilling of His perfect will, which leads to perfect peace. God is not any less powerful if Paige would have died. We are in a fallen world, and the Bible clearly tells us that "in this world, we will suffer" (John 16:33). He says that "it will rain on the just and the unjust" (Ephesians 6:11–18). Why do we only want to pull out the "feel good" scriptures? The ones that feel good to our flesh. This is why we go through life disappointed in God, believing He is not real or faithful when we are holding Him to our word and not His. This life on this earth is a spiritual battle, and there will be tragedy and pain. There is no way around it. Our true reward is not here but in heaven. The sooner we embrace that, the sooner we will walk in peace and in His will.

Once I released Paige to the Lord, I instantly felt at peace. No, I didn't have a different report from the doctors, but I still had peace. I remember standing over Paige as she lay in ICU on life support. I remember it like it was moments ago. It was the middle of the night, and I was standing over her, thinking about what was going on. At that moment, the Lord spoke to me clear as day, and this is what He said. He said, "Satan tried to take her life, and I said no." I can't tell you what this did to me, my spirit, and this entire situation. The Lord told me in this one statement just how powerful He is. He did not have to argue with Satan or struggle with Satan. He didn't even have to bargain with Satan. All He had to say was *no*. Do you know why? Because the battle has already been won. It was won on calvary. Satan already knows he's defeated. He must fall in line with God's will.

So, you might say, "Why do some live and some

die?" "Why is there so much pain in this world?" "Why are so many children abused and hurt?" I don't have all the answers, but I will say this, "God makes no mistakes." Whatever He allows aligns with His perfect plan. Every disappointment, every death, every broken heart, etc., has already been infiltrated into God's perfect plan for your life and His will for your life. Can you accept that? I'm sorry, but that's the truth. We see with our carnal eyes and finite minds. We try to understand when the Bible clearly tells us that "we will not clearly see until we get to heaven" (Corinthians 13:12). I believe (just my belief) that God removes many from this world so that they won't have to suffer. We can't understand that because, again, we are going by what we see and feel and trying to understand by looking at one piece of the puzzle. We are responding to the pain of losing someone that we love. In our minds and emotions, this just doesn't seem right, fair, or that a loving God would allow such pain.

Trusting Him doesn't mean children won't die and that there won't be tragedy in this world. It doesn't even mean that we will understand. What it does mean is that if we live in God's will, we will have more peace knowing that no matter what we see or feel or try to understand, He has our best interest at heart, and at the finish line, it is all for the best and aligning to His perfect "will." Let me repeat, just because we pray daily to stay in His will doesn't mean when the trials and tragedies occur, we won't hurt, but only that Christ will walk through it with us.

OUR PAST

I believe that our past does a lot of damage to our future. Not just in the sense of the consequences of our past but mentally and, even more so, spiritually. I will follow up and say that our omnipotent Savior is aware of all of our mistakes prior to us making them. He still calls us, justifies us, and loves us so much. The Lord has so much love for us that He has made a pathway, even in the midst of our mistakes. How many of us know how to love like this? How many of us, when someone hurts us over and over again, continue to love them, and then, when they come back after all of the damage is done, welcome them with open arms? The Lord lets us know in the Bible that He forgives us for every sin when we are in Him. He also tells us that "grace is not a license to sin" (Romans 7), meaning we don't keep waddling in the same sin, day after day, year after year, just because we live in Christ and He offers us grace when we fall. I guess the real question is, "Are we living for Christ, and is Christ truly in us if we are so comfortable in sin?" From my experiences and reading the Word, I have come to believe that we may die struggling with a sin, but that is the part that we often forget (struggling).

There are things in my past that I don't even know if I will bring myself to put in this book. The Lord is the sole entity who is directing me to write this book. I yield myself to Him and what He wants to be revealed. I have learned that pride is worth nothing. The more and more I live, I realize that if we do not prepare for eternity here, our life is worth nothing, no matter how good we are or any of the good deeds we do. The Lord says our good deeds mean nothing without Him (Ephesians 2:8-9). Let me be clear in saying that as we follow Christ, we will do good works for His glory. This is the evidence of a relationship with Christ, but it is not what saves us. If the Lord directs me to reveal some of my "skeletons" in this book, and I'm embarrassed or shamed, but it leads someone to Christ and glorifies Him, it's worth it. I'm hoping He won't ask me to do it, though.

We seem to always put on such a façade for those around us. This transcends into our jobs, our marriages, and even our relationships with our children. When I was growing up, my adoptive parents always wanted us to look perfect. They always told the perfect stories about us. When we made mistakes, they were not to be spoken of. My sister became pregnant in high school, and they were so embarrassed. They were more concerned about how they would look to people than how my sister was doing, feeling, or why this happened. The pain and disappointment that she must have endured had to have been the worst imaginable. We must understand that many times if we don't get past the emotional and spiritual consequences of our sins, we will not be able to accomplish what God has ordained for us to accomplish. Furthermore, the damage of the sin will be ongoing.

God tells us that we all were born for a purpose (Proverbs 16:4), and that purpose is to glorify Him in our works. We can obtain all the status in this world and leave great legacies for our children and beyond, but if Christ is not in it, it is worth nothing, absolutely nothing. I am saddened that it took me to have tragedies, age, and so much pain in my life to understand many of these principles. I, too, sought after the world's approval and displayed myself in a way that wasn't authentic. When I was alone, the truth of who I truly was and how I felt about myself was ever-present. I just slept it off, drank it off, or drugged it off.

I see celebrities and famous people who are great in this world, and when they die, everyone says that they are in heaven now. As a matter of fact, most people say that everyone goes to heaven, and that's not biblical (Matthew 7:21-23).

Furthermore, the Lord tells us that few will find the narrow pathway into heaven (Matthew 7:13). I knew a man that worked with me who died. I mean, I didn't know him personally, but I knew of him. He was out running on a beautiful sunny day. He came home, had a heart attack, and died. When he died, he died suddenly, and everyone was sad, but the next week I found out that he was an atheist, and I couldn't sleep for almost a week. Not only was he an atheist, but he also didn't want to have anything to do with church or God, and he didn't want his children to either. I would hear people say, "He's in a better place now." No, he's not. He will forever be tortured, and there is no deliverance from that. How can that not make a Christian hurt to the core of their soul, especially those who were close to him? How can we not feel some sense of responsibility when someone we know dies who doesn't know Christ? The thought that this "successful" man with all this world had to offer died and would spend eternity in hell just wouldn't let me rest. I'm saddened beyond measure. Many people said, "Let's pray for his soul."

No, there is no praying for anyone's soul when they die. It is finished. If they have not accepted Jesus Christ, they will spend eternity in hell.

Stop and think about that for a moment. I know that everyone will not receive Christ, but if we haven't tried to introduce Him, how can we be okay with that? I have a coworker now who doesn't believe in God or any god. He said that if I could prove it to him, he would accept it. He said that he is open-minded about it, but at this time, he doesn't believe. My prayer is that God will move on his heart as only God knows how to. I told my coworker, "God will reach you," and I am convinced He will. See, we just need to go and ask God to move in someone's life. We can't tell Him how, but ask Him to move as He sees fit. Our job is to plant the seed. The Lord will do the watering of it.

Maybe that means that person must hit rock bottom, suffer, or endure pain. I know we don't want our loved ones to suffer, but wouldn't it be better for them to suffer for a season than for eternity? I know this is very hard to understand, but we must think in terms of eternity, not just our earthly time here. I think some of us, me included, are so comfortable being here that we forget that this is not our home. I believe that the mere thought of eternity is so overwhelming, even for Christians. We would just rather live our lives in a "good" way, say we believe in Jesus, say some prayers, and when we die, believe that we will just enter into the kingdom. Unfortunately, as I read the Bible, that is not what I read or understand. The Bible tells us, "Even the devil believes" (James 2:19), so how can it be just about believing?

It can be scary when we start talking about walking in what God ordained for us. It's scary to our flesh because we know our flesh can't accomplish God's work. When the Lord told me to write this book, I ignored Him and even laughed. I said, "Who me? The one who has made so many mistakes. "Would anyone listen to anything I have to say?" The Lord reminded me that He would "use the weak things in the world to shame the wise" (1 Corinthians 1:27). On the days that I write, the words just come pouring out. What I learned is that when we yield to the Lord according to His "will," it is not difficult. The Lord says He is "seeking those that he can use" (2 Chronicles 16:9). Once He finds that person, and they yield, I believe the rest is easy. The hard part is Him finding someone to do His will and then that person yielding and not being stagnant in fear.

When we understand that when we are in God's will, He takes responsibility for the outcome, we don't have to worry about it. When we look at it that way, it takes away the fear. Why do we fear? Fear of failing or being embarrassed. All that is pride. What I fear more than anything on this earth is dying, going to heaven, and having the Lord tell me to come in and show me what He had for me to do. Then, He would tell me that He had to have someone else do it because I was too busy with me and my agenda or I was just too afraid. I think about that all the time. I think that is why I was afraid when I was faced with death during COVID-19 (I will speak on that later).

Most, if not all, of the times that I sit down to write this book, I don't even know what I am going to write about. I can only yield my talents to Christ to work through me. I don't worry about the outcome. I have heard the Lord repeatedly telling me to "write the book." I know it's Him, and most of the time, I listen and start writing, and sometimes, I try to ignore it. Maybe that's why the Lord chose me for it. My children and most of my friends tell me I have no filter. Maybe God needed someone who didn't have a filter so He could just speak to and through me. I have been known to say anything. I have learned through this entire book-writing experience that we all have a talent that can be used by God, but it can also be used in the world and not bring Him glory. The gifts of the Lord are without repentance (Romans 11:29). Many people in this world who are famous or we look up to have God-given talents. Most are just using them in the world and not for the Lord.

I just want you to seek your purpose on this earth. Not only because it is pleasing to God, but you will find a place of peace that you will never know walking in your own will. The world's success is not always, and rarely is, the success God has for you. The world's success usually involves money and things, and it is not saying that God doesn't give us these things, but hear me when I say this, "God will not give you things if you can't handle them." The people that have things and God hasn't given them to them, these things destroy them. Why are there so many "famous and rich" people committing suicide, getting divorced, having children being wayward, etc.? It's because they couldn't handle the "things." The things became their god. It doesn't matter how good something is; if it comes before God, then it is your god. This can cover relationships (even our children), careers, money, and so much more.

What's more surprising to me is that even though we all see the destruction of those "famous, successful" people, we still strive for that place. I have learned firsthand that the enemy knows we have weaknesses, and he has no new tricks up his sleeve. He will draw us in with our hearts' desires and tell us that they are not bad. On the surface, they may not be bad, but if it isn't what God has for you or the Lord has told you not to move towards something, and you do, it's wrong and will not turn out well. Then, once Satan has drawn us in, he destroys us. Not only does he destroy us, but he will also take those around us. I believe many of us can look back and see incidences of this in our past. Some of this destruction has lifelong consequences. Again, this goes back to us wanting temporary pleasure and not seeking God (those that are Christians) for His will. When I was married for the first time, I hadn't known my husband very long. When we met, he was very charming, had lots of money, and treated me like a queen. I fell into the trap.

I ended up getting pregnant. I was brought up that you don't have a baby out of wedlock, so we decided to get married. By the time I was three months pregnant, our relationship had begun to fall apart. It wasn't fun or fulfilling anymore. He wasn't treating me as a queen anymore, and I began to find out that all of the money that he made was not made legally. Though I was obviously not living for Christ at the time, I knew Him from the past, and I had heard Him speak to me before. By the time we were going to get married, our relationship was a big mess, but I still married him because I was pregnant. I knew when I was saying my vows I shouldn't have been marrying him. We went on to have another child and ended up divorcing in a very bad way. My children and I paid the price for my disobedience.

Once we commit a sin, we feel like we have to fix it. In reality, the Lord is always there waiting for us to turn to Him, even when we do wrong. We have this sense that if we disappoint God or step outside of His will, that's it, and we are on our own. This is a lie from the pit of hell. When we fall, the Lord wants us to run into His arms so He can help us. Please know that Satan will buy you and give you things to make you happy but understand "being happy" is temporary. Peace is long-lasting. Happiness is based on a thing or situation. Peace is based on the resting place inside you that is always settled no matter what you have or your situation. The enemy used my insecurity issues to draw me into sin. This is another reason that we have to allow God to permeate every area of our mind, body, and soul. He can strengthen those areas where we are weak so we are stronger in times of temptation.

Let me clear something up. We cannot defeat Satan on our own. This is not to exalt him because he is defeated, but only in the power of God's might by His Son Jesus' blood. You cannot outsmart the enemy, and you cannot avoid his traps on your own. This is why we have to pray daily and ask God to give us the wisdom that we can use for Him to help us. When we get to heaven, we will see all of the situations and pitfalls that the Lord helped us to avoid. If you put yourself in Satan's playground, you will lose. There are no "ifs," "ands," or "buts" about it. He will devour you. He doesn't care about your feelings, your past, or your shortcomings. He has no mercy.

I want to ask that if any of you have areas in which you know you are weak, give them to the Lord. It could be insecurity, drugs, hatred, racism, sex, and the list goes on. He already knows about it, but there is something about bringing these weaknesses and struggles to His feet that allows His power to help us. I often pray that God looks into me deeper than I can see and reveals weaknesses in me. I no longer see weakness as being weak, if that makes sense. Jesus tells us that when we are weak, He is strong (2 Corinthians 12:10). We are in a fallen world, and we were born into sin. Most of us were brought up in

dysfunctional environments and had a mirage of hurts, pains, and deceptions to work through.
Many are not of our own doing, and some are. They are both the same to our merciful Savior. He wants them all.

THIS PLACE IS NOT OUR HOME

This is going to be a very difficult chapter for many. This world caters to our flesh, whether it be through pleasure or pain. Eternity is dealing with our spiritual well-being, which many, including myself, don't take care of. We must. Why? Because this is what will last forever. This flesh will be gone, and we will be left with the core of our spirit. We don't like to think about that because that is way too "deep," and that would cause us to change and be uncomfortable. There is no way to transition into what God needs us to be without pain or uncomfortability. Why? Because we have gotten used to making our flesh comfortable. It's kind of like a diet. When we are used to eating anything we want, even though it's not good for us, it is very difficult to start eating healthy foods. I am very athletic in the sense that I work out every day. I would say it is borderline obsessive. When I first started working out, it didn't feel good, but once I realized that I could control how I looked by how much I worked out, I was all in. I also know that physical activity works wonders on how you feel and releases stress.

When I was younger, I ate whatever I wanted and worked out, and always stayed fit. Now, I have to eat half way decent if I want to stay in great shape. I don't like it and don't always do it. In walking with Christ, we must deny our flesh (Matthew 16:24), and that hurts like crap. In this same scripture, He also tells us that "we have to take up our Cross." For a long time, I didn't know what that meant. In the days that we now live, it is crystal clear. The world, as a whole, doesn't follow Christ. This is becoming more and more evident as time goes on. Though we are called to love everyone, we are now having to stand up for the truth. We can no longer, as true followers of Christ, blend in with the world. This can be a lonely place, and you have to be okay with that.

I love the Lord so much, but there are still places in me where I have not given God full control. Why? Because it hurts too bad. This world has gotten to a point where we continually feed our flesh. Whatever we want to do, we do. It feels good at the time. I heard a pastor say something so true a while ago. He said, "The closer you get to Christ, the more sinful you will feel." He is correct, and the closer I get to Christ, the more the world has nothing for me. I can have times of enjoyment with family and friends, but I always have a consciousness of Christ, and that brings me so much peace and, hopefully, to Him so much gladness. Many compare our relationship with Christ to our relationships with our children. Don't you want your children to do the right thing and make good decisions? And if they mess up, aren't good parents there to redirect them but also offer love and forgiveness? Yes, and that is exactly how our heavenly Father is but on a much deeper level. He only wants our love. He is not asking for us to be perfect, and He definitely knows we will make mistakes. But when we do, He wants us to come to Him and repent, receive forgiveness, and turn from our sins. There are many things in the Bible that are crystal clear.

There are many that I know I won't have clarity until I get to heaven. The things that are clear truths, and truths the Holy Spirit has revealed to us, must be acknowledged and walked in. Let me give you a comparison of these two truths. I believe the Word is very clear about "though shalt not murder" (Exodus 20:13, KJV), but maybe not so clear about drinking. For many years, I have enjoyed wine and alcoholic drinks and never felt convicted. About a year ago, the Lord took the taste away, and I never wanted to have a drink. Is drinking itself wrong? I would not say that this is clear in the Bible, but for me, the Lord has removed it and does not want me to partake in it. These two things are the difference between having clarity in the Word and the Holy Spirit giving you a directive that might not be spelled out so clearly in the Word. In this world, as we live now, many sins that are very clear in the Word are being looked at as not being a sin. Many of us Christians have either lost our moral compass in Christ, or we want to fit in so bad that we are quiet about such sins. There will come a day when we will have to stand on one side or the other.

GETTING ANGRY WITH GOD

I was speaking with a close friend of mine last night. This friend has been having a very difficult time financially for a very long time (about three-plus years). She is frustrated and has shared with me that she is trusting God month to month. When I spoke with her last night, she was tired, and understandably so. Financial strain is very difficult to succumb to for a long period of time. She began to say that she was getting angry at God, and then she caught herself as if to stop herself from committing the ultimate sin. I told her to go ahead and say it. I told her, "God is a big boy, and He can take it." I have learned on my journey that God wants a "true" relationship with us.

Listen, there is nothing that we can hide from our Lord. Nothing that we do, and nothing that we feel. He says He knows our hearts and thoughts better than we do (1 Chronicles 28:9). We have this understanding of God that He is sitting on a throne somewhere, and when we come to Him, we must use big fancy words for His Lordship. Yes, we need to honor God, but honoring God is more in how we live and love than how we communicate with Him. When my daughter was dangling between life and death, there were times when I had no words. I could only say the name of Jesus, and sometimes, I could just moan. Do you think God knew what I was trying to communicate? Of course, He did. He knows my innermost thoughts.

What I am saying is that He knows what we are feeling without us saying a word, so we should just go ahead and get it out (it makes us feel better), and then we can deal with it with the Lord. God understands all of our frustrations and pains (Psalm 139:3). He desperately wants us to come to Him for everything. Not just the big things or the little things, but all things. Spoiler alert, there are no big and small things for our Lord. They are all easy for Him because He only has to speak, and it's done. We have to get out of this earthly mindset when dealing with God. He tells us that our warfare is spiritual, not worldly (2 Corinthians 10:4), and we must fight them as such.

I want you to hear me when I say this: "God is not Santa Claus or a genie in a bottle." No matter what your church may tell you, God is not a "name it and claim it" God. He doesn't bow down to our every wish and desire, forgoing His own. I want you to reread that and think about it for a moment. So many people have walked away from their faith because they have asked God to do something, and He didn't, and they feel like He is either a liar or nonexistent, and He is neither. As I spoke about in my earlier chapter, God's "will" will always prevail. God has a purpose and a plan, and it will be fulfilled on this earth, no matter how dismal it looks. What we must understand is that we only see a part of the puzzle, and God sees the entire, finished picture of the puzzle. Let me give you an example. You have a child, and the child gets ill and dies. You have prayed and prayed and believed that God would heal your child. God did heal your child, the ultimate healing. I know we don't want to hear that, but you will not know until you get to heaven the entire picture of what your child would have gone through if God hadn't removed them from this world. You don't know what other factors were altered because of that child dying.

You may say, "It's not fair," but it's God's will, and it is the best. I promise. So, you may ask, "How is that parent supposed to get over the pain?" I promise God has a plan and a ram in the bush for that. We are in a fallen world, and there will be pain in this world (Romans 5:3–4), and it will rain on the just and the unjust (Matthew 5:42–45). That pain may be financial, physical, losing a child, etc., but with Christ, all things are possible, and He will sustain us as we go through it. I am not here to belittle losing a child. I use this as a reference because it is the worst pain that I feel a human could suffer on this earth. Losing a child cuts at the heart of a parent. Have you ever been around a parent who has lost a child? When they cry, it is like no other cry you have heard. It comes from the depth of their soul. Even in that, the Lord can turn it around for good.

If you must get mad at God, go ahead, and tell Him how angry you are. Isn't this what a true relationship is about? Telling someone how you feel about any situation without the fear of losing their love or relationship. I believe it is hard for us to fathom this type of relationship because there are not many of those on this earth. Even with marriage, if one person does this or that, it's over. If a person is struggling with feelings that they shouldn't, they are ridiculed and not looked at the same. Whatever you do, do not leave Him out of the process, no matter how ugly that process is. No matter how angry, disappointed, depressed, and so on. He will get you through it. He will love you through it. In the end, I promise, your relationship will be stronger.

THE LORD'S WILL?

I was perplexed by the scripture that "we receive not because we ask not" (James 4:2). I said, "Well, God, if You are going to do Your will anyways, why even pray? Let's just wait to see what Your plan and will is." The Lord opened a revelation (I love it when He does that). He said that we are to pray in all things, and His "will" will be done, but if we don't pray, we could miss out on the revelation of His will and the peace going through it. Our peace will line up with His will. This scripture does not mean what it has been taught from many pulpits. This scripture talks about the motives that we have when we ask God for things. He is saying that we receive not because when we ask, we ask with wrong motives. I believe this is one of the hardest truths for Christians to embrace. Humans, naturally, want to be in control. We plan our days, months, and even our lives. Many times, without consulting with God. This, coupled with not knowing what God's will is, makes for a lot of confusion. I will say it's a little difficult. I have heard the Lord's voice (again, not audibly), and I have sought Him in a situation and heard nothing.

Many times, when I hear nothing, I stand still, and He either sends me a sign or opens a door so that it can be clear. This takes patience, and I am not sure about you, but this is not my strongest attribute. For some issues, if I need a quick answer, I do an inventory of my heart. What do I mean by this? Is something I am doing done out of love, or is it done out of spite? Once I pass that test, if the decision doesn't make or break anything that I know of, I will make the decision. Let me give you an example. So, say I see someone in need, and I can meet that need. Many will say that it is not always God's will to meet that need. I am typically going to meet that need, as long as it can't cause damage if I am wrong because I would rather be wrong and bless someone than not bless someone, and I should have. That is an example of making an immediate decision without having God's answer.

Now, say I want to purchase a new home, but I'm not sure if I should. I am going to seek God until I get an answer because He and only He knows what tomorrow brings, and I don't want to make a decision that will hurt or bankrupt me later. I will wait until the Lord gives me at least one confirmation, but usually, more than one. I don't want to make big decisions that affect the future without the Lord directing me.

SPIRITUAL AMNESIA

I will say that by far, the miracle that God did by healing my daughter was the greatest miracle that I have witnessed by Him (or so I thought). All of the doctors, and I know many of our friends, didn't think Paige would make it. I would see the looks on their faces when they came to see us in ICU when she was in a coma. I could tell that many, though they loved us and loved the Lord, just thought this was either too hard for God or just not His will. So, I will say again this was the biggest miracle that I saw God orchestrate. There were times when I was going through this journey at the hospital when I could almost feel God's presence. I literally was at the point where I was more peaceful at the hospital than when I was not. I know it sounds crazy, but again, this is the intent of this book to try and communicate the spiritual lessons that I have learned.

Did I have moments where I felt sad and overwhelmed? Of course, but those times were few and far between. I saw nurses, doctors, and other patients and visitors witness God's miracle. Not that I just said it was a miracle, but the doctors and nurses said it was a miracle. He was glorified in front of everyone. It has been seven years, and

I promise, if Paige or I would call up to that ICU and speak to one of those nurses or doctors, they would be in tears and celebrate and praise God all over again. I know because we have. I have come to a place where I absolutely love when I see others see the glory of God. I know it makes God happy, and in turn, it makes me happy. It seems like so many are just living life without a consciousness of Christ that when I see a miracle that is seen by many, it is a huge spiritual celebration. I feel like shouting, "Look what my Daddy did."

Being a single mom for most of my children's lives was not an easy task, though looking back, I see where God made it easier. There were times that I wondered how I would make ends meet. Don't get me wrong, as a real estate agent, I made very good money, but many times was not the best steward of it. That would be an entirely different chapter. My point is there were times, especially now with both kids in college, when I didn't have enough to pay all the bills and the tuition. Many times, I would panic and say, "OMG, what am I going to do?" What a joke. My Father in heaven snatched my daughter from the grips of death itself, and a few years later, I'm wondering how I'm going to make it. Shame on me.

Why do we forget what God has done for us in the past? Why do we think God has somehow lost His power once He performs so many miracles? I am not sure. Maybe, we don't feel worthy, even though God tells us that He is faithful even when we are not (2 Timothy 2:13, NIV). Maybe we think it's not His will to give us the outcome that we want. Hmmm, that's a good one, and one that goes back to my earlier chapter. His "will" is the best, and we will find peace in His "will." As we spoke about, humans want to be in control, so they want to know God's plan and will.

Truth be told, if we knew half of the things we would go through in this life, most of us would probably have jumped off of a bridge a long time ago. Many times, we must be honest and say that we don't trust and wait on God because we are not sure how, when, or if He will work everything out. I try not to worry about the future. The Lord tells us that tomorrow has enough worries on its own (Matthew 6:34). We cannot lose focus on that. This is a daily focus and refocus. Trusting God is a daily focus because we look all around and see so much negativity and destruction, and we sometimes wonder how God fits into all of it. Trust me, He is there, and He has not lost His power and is always ready and willing to work it out for us. Lastly, remember He sees the puzzle and is continually putting those pieces together.

Let's not get spiritual amnesia. When we go through a valley or trial, let us focus on the past trials that God has brought us through. Did I say it would be easy? Sometimes, it will not, but I promise it will be okay. He's got you, just like He had you before.

THE JOURNEY IS LONG

I have gained a lot of respect for authors. Writing a book is not easy, especially when it's your first one. When I first started writing this book, directed by the Lord, I didn't think it would be easy, but I also didn't think that it would take me on the emotional journey that it has taken me on. In writing this book, many emotions have surfaced that I thought were gone or buried so deep as not to affect me. Maybe that's part of His plan. Again, I am acting in obedience and know nothing of the outcome. What I have learned is that this journey here on earth seems long.

Right now, the world is in the middle of a pandemic called the coronavirus disease. It is a virus that is attacking anyone and everyone. People are dying by the thousands, and the doctors have no control over it. The world has essentially been shut down to try and control this pandemic. It will surely be in the history books so you can read all about it. When you go through uncertain times, you begin to really look at life and what lies after. I started thinking about my life. I began looking at how selfishly I live. My job, my kids, my finances, and my friends. I get up every day with my own agenda. Very seldom do I consult the Lord; I just trust that He's got me. And you know what? He does, but what am I missing?

My biggest fear is that I will get to heaven and the Lord will show me the plan He had for my life, and I missed it. I totally missed it. How did I miss it? By daily, monthly, and yearly focusing on me and mine. Then, one day, you realize you are older, and maybe your health begins to fail. Maybe you don't have the energy you once had. You used all your vibrancy on your own agenda, and most of these things have not brought you peace or true joy but temporary happiness. It is so sad. It is sitting heavy on me right now, and it's not the first time. I think about giving it all to God and totally going after His agenda, and then I get sidetracked with my agenda, or maybe I'm scared that He may take too much.

Whatever it is, many of us are going to make it to heaven, but will He be pleased with our race? Will He be able to say to us, "Well done, my good and faithful servant"? That is so sad for us because I know that in His will is total peace and rest. We struggle on this long journey down here on earth, mostly because we are not walking in His will. We are missing out on so much. The basic truth is that either the enemy is keeping this truth from us, or we are just blinded by the treasures of this world.

If we would embrace Christ in this life and allow Him to lead us, life wouldn't be so difficult here, and we would walk graciously and peacefully into His will and purpose.

AND THEN CAME THE PANDEMIC

It has been a moment since I have written. A lot has gone on, and I have been a little disobedient in my diligence in writing. That's one of the reasons that I couldn't believe God wanted me to write this book. I have such a heart for God but fail at so much, and He still blesses me and chooses to use me. Why? Your guess is as good as mine. That will be one of the first questions I ask Him when I get to heaven, amongst a long list of others. Sometimes, serving God and following His will seems so hard, but once you do it, it brings an overabundance of peace that you ask yourself, "Why did I procrastinate?"

So, back to the pandemic. No one has all the answers right now, and I'm sure by the time this book is published, there will be more truths revealed than what I have to offer. In a condensed version, China had a virus called severe acute respiratory syndrome coronavirus 2 (SARS-CoV-2), which is said to have been transmitted from a monkey. Apparently, China didn't notify us, and now this virus that is killing a ton of people is running wild. That is truly the condensed version. It has become political, and did I fail to mention this is a presidential election year? Put that all together, and it is a nightmare here on earth. Everyone has their opinion of what's truly going on. Some say it's a government-orchestrated ordeal where they are trying to thin out the population. Others are so fearful that they might catch the virus that they haven't been outside in months. And still others, mostly young people, believe it's a joke.

I personally don't know what to believe, but one thing I do know is there is some spiritual warfare going on behind the scenes. As Christians, we must know and understand that no matter what happens on this earth, it doesn't surprise our heavenly Father, who knows and sees all. He is not surprised by the virus, the deaths, the wars, and anything else that goes on here on earth. It's unbelievable how life can change so quickly. I took a break from writing, and I contracted COVID-19. I knew I was sick and went to the ER and urgent care, and both gave me a negative result on the COVID-19 test. Well, on July 29, 2021, I had to be taken by an ambulance from my home to the ER, where my oxygen level was below 70 percent. The doctors came in to speak with me, my son, and one of my dear friends and told us that my chances of making it were slim. I was literally gasping for air and being told to calm down. I am not sure if anyone is aware, but when you can't breathe, you tend to panic, and it is very difficult to calm down, though I did try. I was face to face with death. It was very overwhelming because I truly thought I was going to die, and I was gripped with fear. My son was asked about my will and if I wanted to be resuscitated.

I want to speak to those who feel like they have time to give their lives to Christ and that, on their deathbed, they can accept Cphrist. That is a lie from the enemy. We do not know the time or date of our death. When I was in the ER gasping for air, I couldn't make any decisions. I was not in my right mind. I could barely call out the name of Jesus. I will go even further and say that if you have that attitude of waiting until the last minute to accept Christ, your heart may not be in the right place. When I sat in the ER before I was sedated, I could literally feel the pull of death. What do I mean by that? Well, it wasn't anything weird. I just felt the lack of control of my body, and my lack of oxygen could not have lasted much longer. Believe it or not, I was scared, and I didn't know why. Even through the exasperation of trying to breathe, I knew I was standing at death's door, and I was so scared. I wasn't sure why just yet. I mean, I am a Christian and love the Lord Jesus Christ. Why would I be scared of death? Is everyone afraid when they die? I thought that it would be peaceful dying if you knew Christ.

The last thing I remember saying with the little breath I had left was, "Jesus, where are You?" The next thing I knew, I woke up ten days later in ICU. The Lord Jesus brought me back through yet another storm. I won't go through all of the emotions that I went through, but I will tell you my life is His, totally and completely. I told the Lord that where He needs me and leads me, I will follow. I know that the Lord saved me from this to glorify Him, and glorifying Him is what I will do. I know many people feel this way shortly after a traumatic experience, but it has been over a year since this happened, and I still have the same fight that I want to put forth for the Lord. Every day when I wake up, I want to live my day for Him. I realize that I may not "feel" His presence, but I absolutely know that He is there.

After leaving the hospital, I still had a concern about why I feared dying. Yes, I had lived through this horrific virus, though it was a very long recovery process. For days and weeks, I was still overwhelmed by this fear of death that I had when I was face to face with it. Finally, one day, the Lord shared with me the reason for my fear.

The Lord showed me that I lived my entire life for myself, and if I had been face-to-face with Him, I would have gone to heaven but would not have fulfilled the purpose that He had for me. Just thinking about it now makes me sad. Jesus, the One who gave His life for me, saved my daughter from death, delivered me from breast cancer, and now snatched me from the virus' grip, would have been unhappy when I stood before Him. I have lived my entire life, up until that point, saying I'm a Christian but not walking in His will or power. The Lord speaks of this in 2 Timothy 3:5. He says that many will have the form of godliness but deny the power thereof. He says that we are to turn away from people like I was. Wow. That is very powerful. Am I perfect? No, and never will be, but I am more like Him than yesterday and striving every day. When I fall, I pick myself up and ask the Lord to forgive me. You know what? I am falling less and less, and I give Him all of the glory. There are people in this world who are taking their last breath and do not know Christ. That is not okay.

It amazes me as Christians, including myself, that we get so wound up when something happens as if God didn't know it was going to happen. The Lord has shown me the truth in the scripture that "*all* things work together for the good of those that love the Lord" (Romans 8:28). Do we really believe this? Really? I know many people who have had tragedy in their lives and have become angry at God. I am not judging. This life is hard and throws you some things that can knock the strongest man down. That's why we must trust and believe and remind ourselves daily that "this world is not our home" and God is in control of everything. This is a fallen world. This world has destroyed almost all of what God has given us. We have removed God from this life here in so many ways and wonder why there is such chaos. In a way, it's kind of a good thing that we have hard times here on earth. Maybe that helps us yearn for better.

Maybe all of this is ordained so that heaven will just be that much sweeter. Hey, I am the first to tell you I don't have all the answers. One thing I do know is that God is real. He is so real. Unfortunately, when we as humans don't understand something, we don't believe in it. We can't understand how God works, so it must be fake. We don't understand how God could allow so much suffering. We don't understand how God could allow so much evil in this world and so many innocent people to suffer, hurt, and die. Again, I don't have all of the answers, but I know that one day we will, and until then, I'm trusting

Him every step of the way. I must repeat that the reason that I know God is real is due to my valley experiences. I believe that you can know *of* God and believe in Him, but to truly know Him can only come through a valley experience. We will do everything to stay out of the valley. Hey, I'm first in line. I don't want to hurt or feel any uneasiness. I am the wimpiest of the wimps, but many of you know or will know that life many times doesn't give us a heads up when the valley is coming; it just overtakes us. When I received the call that my daughter was hit by a car and almost died, I wasn't prepared. Who could be prepared? To be totally honest and transparent, I hadn't picked up my Bible in months and probably hadn't prayed in almost that long. Some might ask, can anyone ever be prepared for that call? No, probably not, but if we are in daily communication with God, it might be easier to understand how God wants us to maneuver through the valley. Maybe I'm wrong. All I know is that I completely lost it and didn't even have the words to pray. Many times, I just said the name "Jesus." It's all I could say, but thank God I knew exactly where to go and thank God even more that His mercy is everlasting and He is always there for us, even when we haven't been there for Him. That, my friend, is true love.

Let's talk about that true love. Have you ever thought about God's love? God set us up to be happy and peaceful, and we ruined it (thank you, Adam and Eve), but instead of leaving us in an impossible position, He sent His only Son to pay the debt so that we could be reunited with Him. Let's just look at that one piece. God gave His only Son. Now, if you don't believe in God, you will have an issue comprehending this, but for those of us that say we believe in God and Jesus Christ, this should blow our minds. I have two children, and I wouldn't give their life for the godliest person. I just don't believe I could do it, but for someone who hated me, I definitely wouldn't do it. God gave His Son and allowed His Son to suffer on a level that we will never comprehend so that we could be reunited with Him and have everlasting life. Can we just pause for one moment and take that in?

Okay, now we have the opportunity to be reunited with a heavenly Father who loves us, and some of us don't believe in Him, and many of the ones that do, do nothing much to show it. And He still loves us unconditionally. When I reached out to the Lord in the hospital room, I didn't have to beg Him. He was right there like He had always been. What type of love is this? We don't know that type of love here on this earth. That's why marriages end, families are disconnected, friendships don't last, and so on. We walk away from people when they offend us in the least possible way. We offend God daily, I'm sure I do, and He never turns His back on us. Imagine treating someone like this, who did all this for you, and being treated the way we treat Him. Most of us don't reach out to Him unless we are in dire need of Him. We have tried everything we can to fix a situation, and when it doesn't work out, we ask God to fix it. When I think about how many times I, myself, have done this, it makes me sick. If the Lord never did another thing for me, He has blessed me so far beyond what I deserve.

Most posts I see these days are saying things that have to do with the Lord blessing us. Very seldom do I see posts asking God, "What can I do for You today?" "Who can You put in my pathway today to bless?" "Who is hurting and needs to hear that You love them?" I know, for the most part, that's me. I want that to change, and I believe I am changing through Him. My main reason for wanting the change is because we are most certainly in unchartered times, and most, if not all of us, know that some things are not right and the time of assuredness is over. Most of us know that we are losing control, or the control we thought we had. Even those who have money and the world's riches know that there are outside factors that are affecting our families and us, and we have little to no control. This is scary and makes us very uncomfortable. I know that God needs some helpers down here. Yep, you heard me right; God needs us. He needs our hands, our feet, our eyes, ears, and our voices to warn people. I don't know about you, but I wouldn't even want my worst enemies to experience death without Christ. I don't want them to experience life without Him, but death is even worse because there is no coming back from the eternity that awaits those who do not know the Lord.

Being used by the Lord these days will mean we will be uncomfortable. This will mean going against the grain and sometimes being ridiculed and laughed at. This will also mean that many times you will have to walk alone here on this earth. Some may think you are crazy, but in love, we must try and tell as many as we can about dying without Christ. This doesn't mean that we will have to act like mentally challenged people. The Bible reminds us that they will know us by our love (John 13:35). Let's just start there. I have come to realize that if you never mention the name of the Lord at first with someone and show them love in a world that loves little, they will see something peculiar about you. When I went through my tragedies, there were many people who actually commented that I seemed unbelievably calm going through my situations. This was my opportunity to tell them how the Lord was carrying me through. Since these situations, I have had people call me while going through tragedies or bad situations and have asked me how I got through my tragedies without losing my mind. This is when I can share with them that the Lord gave me daily strength and tell them to ask the Lord, and He will be there. All things are to glorify the Lord. I have no strength of my own. I am the weakest amongst you, I promise. Sometimes our weakness can be a strength in that we call out to the Lord sooner. There are those that have strong wills and the capability to endure many things on this earth. I believe they may get through the tragedies but not with the peace the Lord offers.

JESUS IS COMING BACK, WHETHER WE BELIEVE IT OR NOT

I asked myself, "Why are so many churches not preparing people for Jesus' coming?" Then, I am reminded that "we are the church" (1 Corinthians 3:9). We are the ones that need to do the work of Christ, and He is looking around for *anyone* who will do His will. That person may not be dressed up pretty or smell right. This person may not be educated or articulate. He will use anyone and anything to get His message out. Many who are held up on pedestals in this world will not be used by God. I did not say they could not; I said they will not. This world and its riches have a way of giving people just enough happiness that they don't seek God. Many people that have money and fame will never seek the Lord. Seeking the Lord takes humility, and many who have this world's riches cannot humble themselves.

The greatest gift that the Lord could give someone who has everything in this world is to humble them. Remove the fame and fortune, and therefore, they might cry out to the Lord. Does that seem harsh? No, it does not. I would rather spend eternity with the Lord and suffer in this life than gain all of this world's riches and spend eternity away from the Lord. I mean that from the bottom of my heart. This is why I try and humble myself. When I feel myself getting haughty or feeling like I am great, I stop and step away from life and remind myself of the times when I had nothing and remind myself that I could do nothing without Christ. I want nothing, no matter how bad I want it, if it is not of God. I don't care how much I beg, kick and scream. Please, Lord, don't give it to me. I want to spend eternity with the Lord no matter what it takes and no matter what I have to suffer. I thank the Lord for the tragedies that He has allowed. I wouldn't change one of them.

Many people would say that writing a book isn't easy. Try writing one in the direction of God, not necessarily knowing what He wants to say. Someone asked me, "Why don't you get a ghostwriter?" I said, "The Lord instructed me to write the book." It is now April 17, 2022, and I am still trying to be obedient.

We have all been through a lot these last couple of years. Some more than others. The first thing that I have learned in the last couple of years may not be very popular. It won't be popular because our society, including many of our churches, has led us to believe that our God is a genie in a bottle. The problem with that is when we "rub the genie" and we don't get what we want, we want to blame God. That name-it-and-claim-it mentality is a lie from the enemy and, unfortunately, was cosigned and preached from many pulpits. Telling God what to do is not praying. I have to say that one more time, telling God what to do is not praying. I have learned that the scriptures are right when it says we will suffer in this life. Some will suffer more than others, and that we won't understand until we get to heaven. I have also learned that even unto death, I must trust Him. As we are dealing with life and all that it throws at us, we have no other choice but to know that God is there with us and He will go every step with us and He has a plan. As I shared with my daughter today, we must focus on God and not the journey.

I remember praying years ago, and I was overwhelmed by some situation. Obviously not too important because I can't remember what it was. The Lord said to me that I should focus on Him instead of the issue. He went on to say that this was what He did when He suffered on the cross. He said He focused on us as He endured the pain of the cross. I will never forget that. We must not forget that Jesus had a choice. In Matthew 26:53, we are reminded that Jesus could have called on His Father and legions of angels to pull Him off that cross.

His love for us was greater than His pain. Wow. Let that sink into your heart.

The Lord already has the journey of our life mapped out. He knew about the wrong turns, the disobedience, and the failures. He still had the plan. Most of us spend so much time fearing what could happen we cannot focus on today and what God is doing and wanting to do today. People would say, "Why do we need to pray if God will do whatever He is going to do?" This, again, is one of those thoughts that I can't fully explain, but I have come to understand that when we pray, we unleash God's will. Going back to my daughter's near-death accident, I began to pray for the Lord to heal my daughter on this side of heaven. God knew what I wanted even before I spoke the words. Do you think the Lord didn't know I wanted my daughter to live? He knows all of the desires of our hearts. He did not confirm to me in prayer that my child would live. If my daughter had died, God is still God and still as good. I found my peace once I released my daughter to God.

Back to the genie-in-the-bottle idea, many of us don't want to deal with God if He doesn't do things our way. I am going to put it out there plainly. Many will never serve God because He won't do their will. When we choose our will instead of God's will, we miss out on so much, including His peace, direction, and His accountability for how the situation works out. I know that even if my daughter died, God would have walked me through that valley, and He would have turned it around for my good because I love Him. Many may say, "How can God turn around a death of a child?" I used to ask the same thing when I read the story of Job. This faithful servant had lost so many replaceable things, but when he lost his children, I was also confused about how God could make amends for this. Now, I realize the depth of His power and His love, and I understand it is possible. I understand that it is possible to even endure death and rest in His peace. For those of us who have not totally surrendered to the Lord, this will be near to impossible to accept. Once we have surrendered all of our wills to Him, we will understand that all we have is His, even our children, and that He will truly do what's best, even unto death.

    I am going to say something that might be controversial, but here it goes. I believe that it is worse in this life to believe in God but not surrender and truly know Him than it is for someone who doesn't know Him at all. Why do I say that? I say that because when you know of

God but don't know how He operates and don't 100 percent trust Him with everything, you are constantly living in a state of fear. When we truly rest in Christ, our fear can't stay because He holds the future. When fear tries to creep up, I remind it that the Lord holds my future and the future of those that I love in His hands. Whatever He allows is for the best. When we don't truly believe that and a trial or tragedy comes, we won't give it up to God. We hold on to it and try to work it out ourselves because the thought of God not working it out how we want it is not an option.

KNOWING GOD VERSUS KNOWING OF GOD

What I now know is that we can be a Christian and be at a place of knowing of Christ but not truly having a relationship with Him, and therefore "knowing Him." In these last days, our Savior needs us to know Him and His voice so that we can serve Him and be directed by Him. While we are going around complaining from day to day and asking God to "give me this and give me that," there are those that don't know Christ and are on their way to hell *forever*. Do we really understand that? I was listening to a pastor who really brought it home. He said, "This Christianity thing is getting ready to get real." We can read about Him, go to church and sing to Him, and we can even give in His name, but when the storms are raging, which way will we turn, and will we quickly blame Him for allowing the storm?

Let's go even deeper. Do we trust Him, even unto death? Would you accept it if you were diagnosed with cancer and had two months to live? Sure, I know God can miraculously heal you, but what if it is not His will to do so on this side of heaven? Can you die in peace knowing that God has you, even unto death? Stop, and think about that.

Really, think about it. God is not concerned about us being comfortable but in preparing us to do His will and to help Him in these last days spread the Good News of His love. We spend so much time asking the Lord to bless us with things that have no eternal value. How many of us can say that we daily ask God, "Lord, use me today." The time is so short. It's not enough to solidify our place in heaven. If we really believed in the eternity of heaven and hell, would we be so lax in trying to tell others about their fate?

We are in a time where no one wants to offend anyone. Or maybe I should rephrase that and say that Christians don't want to offend anyone. The world has no issue throwing sin in front of us and almost mandating that we accept it. Some of us just go along with the notion of acceptance, so the boat won't be rocked. There is going to come a time when we will have to take a strong stand for Christ, and it will cost us something, if not everything, on this earth. If we really knew the fate of most, the Word says few will enter in (Matthew 7:14), would we care about being offensive? Even the churches (the building of the church) don't want to offend parishioners for fear that they won't come back to the church or give money to the church. If we really believed in what we preached, would we really care about how much is in the offering, getting a new jet, or walking around in 1000-dollar suits?

Don't get me wrong, there is nothing wrong with having things, but many don't understand that those things aren't their god. The Lord showed me that anything I put most of my energy into is my god. Yes, your children can be your god, and mine were. I had to let go. We need to pray over our children and then let it go. We often look back and say what we could have done better and blame ourselves for our children's misfortunes. That, again, is a lie from the enemy. Satan is the accuser of the brethren (Revelations 12:10). If we truly trust God with our children, then we wouldn't be sitting up all night when they don't come home as I used to. How do we get to this place of trust and peace in God?

I wish that I had a 1-10 steps list to give you, and then it was done. Unfortunately, most of my lessons have come from me taking the hard way, and I don't want you to have to go that route. God doesn't want you to go that route. Most of the time, we must come to the end of our strength to give it to God. It must be something that is totally out of our control before we will give it to the Lord. By that time, we are so worn physically, mentally, and spiritually that the damage to our health has already happened. Even then, we take it back from time to time.

Let me give you an example. At this time, I have a twenty-one-year-old son, Cross, and a twenty-two-year-old daughter, Paige. Paige, for the most part, is a rule follower. She is in her final year of college in Los Angeles, and she makes pretty good decisions most of the time. Though she went through tragedy with her accident, it taught her so much. She spent a lot of time alone, so therefore, she knows how to be alone. She ended up having seventeen surgeries, had to live in rehab to learn to walk again, and finally had to deal with severe PTSD. There were some dark days, but greater were those days when we had overwhelming peace that God was in control. Paige is very grounded. During this time period, Paige and I reached out to God daily, even hourly, because not even I could understand the severity of what she went through. Paige and I both have said many times we wouldn't trade that valley for anything. Paige's relationship and patience with God are unlike any I have seen, even with adults who have walked with the Lord forever. She has learned to trust the Lord, and when He tells her to wait or He tells her no, she may have a short breakdown but always comes around with the fact that she only wants God's will.

Cross is totally different. He likes to live on the edge and bounces to his own beat, and he has a very strong sense of himself. He isn't as focused as Paige, but his heart is pure gold. He is the type of person who would bring homeless people home, feed them, clothe them, and never tell anyone. With Cross living on the edge, I have often stayed up many nights worrying about him. Wondering if he was okay. I would say, "Cross, please let me know when you are going to stay out." Sometimes he does, and sometimes, he doesn't. He also has a sense of humor that is out of this world. I take responsibility that I enabled Cross. I am not sure if any of you can relate, but it is something about those boys. Cross has also taken the brunt of what I call my mistakes (this is me speaking, not God). We need to make sure that we truly pray about who we have children with, and then, that is still not a guarantee. Me, searching for love and marrying his father was not in God's will, and Cross suffered from this in so many ways. Again, the Lord knows how to reach Cross.

The Lord knows how to reach all of our children, even when we make mistakes. Rarely have I found that the Lord can use us to reach our children. We are too close to our children, and it is too difficult for us to allow and sometimes implement the lessons that God must use to reach our children. It's just that simple. Absolutely, we can pray and live out our faith right in front of them, but their decisions of accepting Christ, living for Him, and trying to be like Him is totally their decision. When we have a child that we are concerned about them being on the right path, the only tool we truly have is prayer. We have to pray and truly trust that God will never accuse us or blame us for any mistakes that we feel like we have made with our children.

Any life can be redeemed, and no sin is unforgivable except the sin of blasphemy of the Holy Spirit, which is referenced in Mark 3. Never give up on someone's salvation. As long as someone has breath in their body, there is hope. Now, once there is no breath in their body, there is no hope. There is no praying for their soul. It's a done deal. The Lord will convict us of sin, not bring up our past sins that have been forgiven. Anytime you have repented of a sin, turned from it, or even are still struggling with it, God will not accuse you of the past. He comes to us in love, with open arms, wanting us to live in peace. The Lord doesn't want us to live in bondage to the past. Why would

He? That would mean that what He did on the cross was in vain. He does want us to turn from our sins, but He doesn't want us in bondage from past sins.

We have to pray and truly trust that God will orchestrate our child's pathway. God has a way, as He did with me, of setting up situations at just the right time. He knows how to reach a person's heart and what it will take for them to surrender. I am constantly praying for protection over my children. I am constantly asking the Lord to close doors that He doesn't want my children to go through and so much more. After all the prayers, we have to release them and trust God. I believe that trusting God is something like that old game we used to play. Remember, we would have a friend stand behind us, and we would fearlessly fall backward, trusting that person would catch us. I could never do it because I knew how bad it would hurt if they didn't catch me. With God, we just have to fall into His arms. Just let go. Don't try to work it out anymore. If the Lord wants you to do something, ask Him to make it clear to you. When I had COVID-19 and was taken by ambulance to the emergency room, Cross came ASAP. He was very upset, obviously, that his mother couldn't breathe, and the outcome was questionable. This was at the time that the hospitals were not allowing anyone in as visitors. This was during the delta variant of the virus. When Cross was in the ER with me, they finally told him he had to leave. Cross sat in his car and waited for the hospital nurses' shift to change, snuck back into the hospital, came into my room and put two chairs together, and watched me all night long. I did not know this was happening. I was already out of it by this time. He also didn't tell me about this. A friend told me about this weeks later.

    Cross doesn't always follow the rules, and that scares me, but I also know Cross has a very pure heart and cares deeply for people, especially people that are struggling. This is a heart I know the Lord can use. I would pray and ask the Lord to watch over Cross, direct his path, keep a hedge of protection around him, and I would still worry myself sick. That is not trusting God, and I can't tell you how I crossed over into the true trust. I think I was just tired of worrying and stressing. The Lord reminded me that Cross is His child first. I know we have all heard this, and it is so true. I heard a pastor that went one step further. He said the Lord told him he didn't have to ask him for permission even if He wanted to bring his son home. Think about that. We say, "How can God allow this? He knows I can't go through that." We can get through anything with Christ, anything. We are looking at a very small piece of the puzzle. God sees the entire puzzle and made it and has put it together. That is why we must trust Him, even unto death.

I am going to say one more unpopular thing. We, as Christians, are way too comfortable on this earth. Let me remind us all again that this is *not* our home. We are literally passing through. The Word says our life and time here are but a twinkling of an eye (James 4:14). Why do we hold on so tight to this world that brings us so much hardship and pain when we know we have a perfect kingdom and Father who is waiting on us? We must learn to stay mindful of our journey. I am not saying this is easy, but through our failures and our disappointments in this world, hopefully, we can be reminded of this. I must remind myself many times a day of this, along with many other truths. Many times, I see the world as my reality, but it's not. There is so much more going on than we can see. My brothers and sisters, our feelings and what we want mean nothing when it comes to the kingdom of heaven and what the Lord is doing.

Everyone, again, everyone on this earth will suffer. If all we had was this time on earth, and then it's all over, that's a reason to be depressed and have no hope. What do we truly believe? Let me promise that in these times, your faith is going to be tested. Again, God is not concerned with our comfort on this earth. There is too much at stake. I also grew up with the name-it-and-claim-it way of seeing and understanding God. I remember one time I went to church, and the pastor said, "I know nothing bad will happen to my children because I serve a God that can prevent it, and if He doesn't, I don't want to serve a God like that." This was more than twenty years ago, and I still remember the pastor saying this. Something didn't sit right as this pastor said this. I didn't have the knowledge or past experiences to dispute it, but I knew it wasn't sitting well with my spirit. I later learned that the Lord does hurt when we hurt, but not enough to abort His plan.

The Word says that everything we have gone through will be worth it when we see what God has in store for us (Romans 8:18). When we have the thinking as this pastor, and something happens that we think is not good or doesn't feel good, we quickly blame God and want to back away from Him. Who do we think we are that we should tell the Maker of the universe to do what we say? Again, this is a temporary stay for us, and it is definitely an evil, fallen world that we are a part of. I have learned to enjoy the happiness that I experience here on earth with my family and friends. It definitely makes being here better. I always remember that the happiness that is here is short-lived. People disappoint us knowingly and unknowingly, people die, and many other things happen that can destroy earthly happiness. Again, true joy and peace can only come from Christ Himself.

FEELINGS AND FAITH

I have always been an emotional person, and to be bound by our emotions is very dangerous. Making decisions based on emotions can have lifelong consequences. On the one hand, being emotional allows me to experience happiness at heightened levels, but it also means that my disappointments hit hard. I am not talking so much in this chapter about how we relate to others emotionally in relationships but about the decisions we make dictated by our emotions.

I once heard someone say, "If we ever got our emotions in check, we could overcome almost anything and make the best decisions." Boy, has that been true for me. How many of you have been in relationships that you knew were not healthy, but you loved them so much, or so you thought? How many times have you wished you could take back words spoken? How many times have you made an array of decisions based on what you feel? The list goes on. Our emotions can be key to making a bunch of mistakes that can't be corrected. Most of the major decisions in my early adult life I have made based on emotions, and most of these decisions have been very bad. I say all of this to say that we must be very careful with our feelings and our faith. Some people confuse them as being the same, and they are not. They can actually work against one another and cause a bunch of confusion. There are times that we may want something so bad that we feel like we are walking in faith when we are only enabling our own emotions and what we want.

Let me give you an extreme example. Say you meet someone and fall in love with them, but they are married. You are so overwhelmed with your emotions when there is no way that there is a blessing in that relationship. God will never go against His Word, no matter how much we want it. I know that this was a very extreme case, but other cases, though maybe not as extreme, can cause just as much or more damage in our walk and growth with the Lord. I look at how much time I wasted on holding on to my desires versus seeking God's desires and will for my life, which ultimately is the greatest.

We must get our feelings under control in every area, from our children, marriages, friends, enemies, and so forth. God *never* allows us to hate others for anything. We may feel hatred, but we must pray through that. Let me tell you a story. My first husband cheated on me with someone I knew while I was pregnant with my second child.

My first child was only sixteen months old. When I found out, I lost it. He moved out, and when I said I hated him, it was an understatement. I blamed him for cheating, destroying our family, and in my head, destroying my children's life. I remember saying to many people, including his mother, that I wished he was dead. I meant it with every fiber in my body. My heart was so broken, and what he did was so wrong, and I felt justified on every level for feeling as I did. I wasn't brave enough to carry out this act, but I would have been okay if I had received the call that he was dead. I'm being very honest. One day, as I was driving and crying out to God to heal my heart, I heard Him say, "Pray for him." I said, "No, I am not praying for him." I said, "Let his mother pray for him." For many days and weeks moving forward, I continued to have these same conversations with the Lord. All this time, receiving no relief from my broken heart. One day when the Lord asked me to pray for my now ex-husband, I said, "Okay, I will pray for him, but I don't want to. I am only doing it because You keep telling me to." My prayers started with something like, "Lord, I pray for him." That was it. Then it went to, "Lord, reach his heart." Then, it went to, "Lord, protect him and forgive him because he doesn't know what he has done." Then, one day, I found myself sincerely praying and crying out to God for him. That's when God made the scripture, "obedience is better than sacrifice" (1 Samuel), come alive in me.

See, there will be many things that God will ask us to do, and we don't *feel* like it. Sometimes, we are justified when someone has wronged us. He understands that, but He still requires our obedience. I guess what I am saying is to do it anyway. Ignore your feelings and pain, and just be obedient. Being obedient to God is not going to always mean we are happy about it. We still have to push through our feelings. Believe me, I am not all the way there at this point, but I am learning daily. It can be as simple as taking a shopping cart back to its place. I'm ashamed to say I used to be one of those people who never took their cart back. One day, I heard the Holy Spirit say, "Take the cart back." I'm thinking, *Really, what's the big deal?* I did it and felt that I was obedient. How do we know when we are being obedient? Well, for me, I feel the strong unction of the thing that God directed me to do being released, and I feel a peace that I don't feel until I have done the task. God had to start me out very slowly because I was a mess. Was it a big deal to take my cart back? Well, it wouldn't change the world, but if God asked me to do it, I needed to be obedient. If I wouldn't listen to Him telling me to take a cart back to its place, why would He trust me to do something that has any impact?

My point in all of this is to say once we learn to hear from God, we need to be obedient and leave the consequences to him, kind of like this book. This is all Him, not me. If I do nothing but write it and it never gets to anyone, that's on Him. When we truly give something to Him, it really does make our job easier. When I sit down to write this book, I never know what I am going to write on any given day. I open my computer and say, "Okay, God, what would You like to say?" And then I start typing, and it flows. Now, let's talk about hearing His voice.

HEARING FROM GOD

So, I will tell you that I have never heard an audible voice or direction from God, but I have learned to hear His voice. Maybe He speaks to everyone differently. In my case, I have always been in a calm state. I have always yielded to Him, meaning I would usually be in a place of need or in a place where I wanted to be used by God. When my daughter was in ICU, and I was standing over her, God spoke so clearly to me. He said, "Satan tried to take her, and I said no." The impact of those words almost eight years ago still brings me to tears. He just said no. If someone had to ask me, "How do you know you are hearing from God?" I would have to say it's a strong thought that comes across and is vivid. One time, I was driving, and I passed a homeless man. I had a strong unction or thought to stop and give him some money. I just stopped and gave the man a few dollars to get something to eat.

One absolute rule is God will never tell you to do something bad to someone. He will never go against His word and tell you to do something. I used to tell myself, *What if I am wrong?* The worst is that I have done something nice for someone. I believe that God will honor my heart and that I was trying to do something to honor Him. We don't have to get so deep into "how do I hear from God." My experience is when I am paying attention to God, seeking Him, and spending time with Him, I will hear Him. Another thing I will add is the times that I have heard from the Lord is so monumental I remember them forever. I am not saying that His word was telling me to do anything big, just that hearing His voice made such an impact on me that I always remember whatever it is He said.

I have found that God wants us to be transparent and trust Him with our weaknesses and frailties. I can almost assure you that with all the sounds of the world and our desires, it will be very difficult to hear from God. Part of us hearing from God is yielding and surrendering. We cannot say that we love the Lord and live the way we want, not trying to honor Him. Again and again, I say that we will sin and fall short, but we can't just live in sin and practice sin. The Lord tells us that those who practice sin "will not inherit the kingdom of heaven" (1 Corinthians 6:9-11). I know that this is not a popular and accepted scripture, but it's still true. His Word never changes. No matter what year it is or what the culture has yielded to, His Word and His standards do not change, period.

When I tell you I was a hot mess, I was that and more. I was born to a prostitute and an unknown father. I was then put up for adoption and went from foster home to foster home until being adopted at two and a half years old. I had such a spirit of rejection (I didn't know what that was early on) that I lived a very insecure life until I was about thirty-five years old. I never felt loved by my adoptive parents. At thirty-three years old, I hired a private investigator to find my biological mother, who, when found, didn't want to have anything to do with me. I married a man who was controlling and cheated on me. I came out of that marriage with two children. I made those children my everything because I felt that I finally had something of my own. I, then, almost lost my daughter when she was fifteen, was diagnosed with breast cancer a year after that, and then almost died of COVID-19 last year. Between all these events, there was a mirage of mistakes and sins. At no time did Jesus ever give up on me, ever.

I accepted Christ at a young age but didn't really have a relationship with Him. I just knew that He existed. I am not saying you cannot be saved and know *of* God, but to know God personally, you must visit the valley. In the valley is where you are most vulnerable, you have nothing to lose, and when you seek God with such intensity. I wish everyone could truly see and know of God's true love for us. Many don't, and I believe that it is because there is no such love here on this earth, even close to His. Even when a parent loves a child, it doesn't come close to God's love for us. When you are at your worst, lost in sin, with nowhere to turn, that's when the Lord truly shows us His love in all of its purity. Even when we totally turn our backs on Him, He stands there waiting and wanting us to come back to Him.

Please seek that true relationship with Jesus Christ now. I believe that this is the essence of this book. Ask the Lord to reveal the truth of His love and His calling for your life. Again, there are many who know nothing of Jesus. There are many more that know of Jesus but worship Him from afar. There are so many that are lost, and Jesus wants to use us to spread the Good News. I know that in this world, the Gospel of Christ is not the most popular, but it is beyond necessary. If you don't know how to speak to Jesus, ask Him to help you. I promise that He will direct you, and you will be blown away. Humble yourself before Him and tell Him how you feel. Tell Him you want to know who He truly is, not just what you read about or were taught. I promise you, He will reveal Himself to you.

HIS PEACE BLOWS MY MIND

The Lord tells us that "His peace passes all understanding" (Philippians 4:6), and again, His Word is so true. God's peace feels like a spring day when the weather is about seventy-five degrees with a slight breeze. Even when there are storms and all of the drama that is going on in this world, He has given me (and wants to give you) so much peace. I have never known this type of peace. I have always relied on temporary happiness where there had to be something that made me happy (i.e., a vacation, a guy, a basketball game (I love basketball), money, an event, etc.). Now, when I wake up and go through my day, there is just a joy that I can't explain. Do I have issues that come up throughout the day with work, etc.? Of course, I do, but I have a choice whether to allow those things to take my peace, and the choice is ever-present. Do I always stay in a peaceful place? Absolutely not, but peace is more prevalent than at any other time in my life, and for no other reason except I am excited about Jesus. He has shown me His power and His unconditional love for me, and I believe His Word, and I am excited to be used by Him. I get up most mornings saying, "Lord, what can I do for You today?" And it is exciting to watch Him orchestrate it. Anyone who has truly been used by God can attest to how amazing it is. There is just a joy to know that in the midst of this world and all that is going on, I did something to make the Lord smile.

I also have such a loyalty to the Lord because I know where I was and all the sins that I have committed. I know of all the time that I have wasted, and knowing how fragile life is, I want to get as much done for Him as I can before I leave this earth. It may sound like another cliché, but this world has nothing to offer me anymore. Yes, I enjoy the sunshine and the joys that are here, but it is nothing compared to serving the Lord and knowing that He is pleased. I promise you anything that you have in this world outside of Christ will not last and will not give you longstanding peace. He is our peace, and nothing else can compare. I believe that the reason that the enemy tries and succeeds so much in keeping us from experiencing this joy and peace is that he knows when we truly experience the peace of God, our lives will be forever changed. The enemy knows and fears that if we ever come into God's presence, we will never be bound and entangled by his traps.

Please don't believe you have time because you may not. Please do not stay in your comfortable "bubble" of Christianity. The Lord requires more from us. He requires us to tell the lost about Him and show them the way. He requires us to allow Him to move through us and to draw others in with our love. We can see the destruction in this world, and it will not get any better. We can see where evil is called good and good is called evil; Isaiah 5:20–21 sounds familiar. The Lord said it would happen. Once you die or He comes back, whichever comes first, there is no second chance. Look at those around you that are dying and do not know Christ. Ask the Lord to tell you how to reach them. Please.

I know that we are going to get to a place in this walk here on this earth where our faith is going to be tried to its deepest depth, and I am afraid that many of us will fail. We don't want to offend anyone. We don't want to make waves. How horrible will it be to get to heaven and know that you could have created a pathway for someone else and chose not to for fear of offending them? The time is here when the Lord is calling us to be bold. Not annoying or weird, but bold. I know for a fact that if you ask Him to open the doors to share Him, He will.

LIFE IS HARD

Let's face it, no matter how strong we are as a person, life is hard. Yes, there are those enjoyable times when you feel happiness to its fullest, but life always has a way of presenting something that can knock you off your feet. I heard a pastor say once, "If you are on the mountaintop, enjoy it, but don't worship it, because there will be another valley. And, if you are in the valley, pray through it and don't get discouraged because there will be another mountaintop." I find this to be so true of life as I get older. I think when we are younger, we have a warped view of life. We feel like we can plan out our life, who we will marry, how many children we will have, where we will live, and the list goes on. The reality of it is we have no clue what it takes to weather the storms of life.

I remember when I first became pregnant, I said, "I will never put my children in front of a television to distract them." Well, low and behold, Barney was their best friend. I now understand that it is okay to plan, but when we are in Christ and living for Him, we must be flexible. I have come to know now that the closer I get to the Lord, the clearer I hear His plan, and it then becomes my plan. Not just because I changed my mind but because I began wanting and even craving after His will. When I don't know God's will, I can become frustrated, which is not good either. I am learning patience, and I am learning that this life is not my own. It was paid for with a dear price and therefore is owned by God. I believe heaven is where we will have unlimited fun and peace. I just pray that there is food and that sweets are not bad for you. Sorry, that was a sidebar. For now, the battle is intensifying here on earth.

My dear friend, when you feel weak, you must stop and ask God to carry the load. I now know that when I become overwhelmed, it's because I am carrying something I am not supposed to or I am out of God's will. But do not neglect praising Him all of the time, regardless of the situation or your feelings. The closer we get in relationship with God, the harder it will be to ignore His will. There are now places that I have no desire to go and things I used to do that I have no desire whatsoever. I don't even think that I made a conscious thought not to do these things; I just don't want to.

I don't want you to ever think that you are weaker than anyone else or you should be stronger. God never meant for us to carry a lot of what we carry. We choose to carry these heavy loads.

Even when we put ourselves in situations that are difficult, He is right there to help us and show us a new way, so we don't keep heading toward destruction. How the Lord's heart must hurt watching us make mistakes over and over again that hurt us. He is standing there saying, "Trust Me, follow Me, I have a better plan and path for you." Think about people who live their entire life not knowing of His love, grace, and peace and then die. I hate that for me it took so long to understand this. I look back at all the many mistakes that I made, over and over again, and I wonder what God could have done through me in that time. The Lord showed me that even in that regret, it's not of Him. The Lord knew every mistake that I would make, and He knows every mistake that you have made and will make. He still loved and called you. How do we get through these obstacles, tragedies, and inconveniences of life? Nothing and no one but Christ. Will it always be easy? Again, no, but you will get through them, and He will restore anything and anybody that was lost. He will give you His strength so that you can be stronger and go further than you can on your own. When we use our strength to get through situations, sometimes we get through them, but even if we do, it's harder, the scars are greater, and the end result is not God's best.

So, let's recap. Everyone will suffer here on this earth. There is no way around it. God is not a genie in a bottle. We don't just tell Him what we want, and He gives it to us. This is what is frustrating to us and why we doubt God and His faithfulness. We believe that if God doesn't do what we ask, He's wrong when we rarely stop and seek His will. As difficult as it is for us to understand and accept, God really does know best and wants the best for us. I didn't say that it feels the best all of the time, but it is the best. Let me give you an example. All the disappointments and tragedies in my life have not felt good. Many were beyond gut-wrenching and painful. All of this pain has made me who I am, and after the Lord turned it around and worked it around in me, it has made me strong, and I walk in boldness and can speak to others that have tragedies with truth.

I did not say God orchestrated these painful things, but He allowed it because He, in all His wisdom, knows what it will take to make me usable for Him. I think the real devastation is when we go through tragedies and pain and we don't turn to Him. Then, we are left with our own devices to get us through. We end up damaged and bitter. When we finally get to a place of trust in God, we accept anything that comes at us as His will. No, it won't feel good, but if we remember whose we are and that He is with us and is allowing us to go through this, it takes some of the pressure off. This is a process. It comes from practice and more practice. I wish I could say I was all of the way there; I'm not, but I am so much closer than I used to be. Sometimes, things will come at me, and I will just react before I think about praying, "Lord, help me." Why? Because we are trained to react in our flesh, so we have to retrain our flesh, our mind, and our habits.

I am so grateful for the Lord's patience with us. We often say, "I am waiting on the Lord." Well, I promise, He has waited on most of us much longer than we wait on Him. It's sad that it takes most of us to come into a real tragedy or come to the end of our strength and resources before we call on Him. The One that loves us more than anyone. Again, I think that is because we are prone to our senses of "touch, feel, hear," and since He doesn't come at us that way, we believe He's not with us. I promise you, as a witness, that if you ask the Lord to reveal Himself to you, He will. He is not playing games with us. We are just in such a place in this world where we can't hear God because of all the distractions. When I was in the ICU, not knowing if my daughter would live or die, I cried out to the

Lord, and once I surrendered my will, His presence was felt immensely. When I said I had more peace in that hospital after turning the situation over to God than I had ever had before it happened. Why is that? Because the Lord came running when I cried out to Him. I ask you right now to cry out to the Lord and just ask Him to make Himself real to you. He is true to His Word, and it will not return void (Isaiah 55:11). Before you call out to Him, make sure that you are ready to let Him fix you, heal you, and guide you. He knows every pain and sore spot you have. He wants to heal them, but He needs you to invite Him in. Do not tell God what you want to be done; ask Him to do what He knows needs to be done. Your way hasn't worked. You have tried, and where has it gotten you?

If you take nothing else from this book, whether you be fifteen or ninety-five, you still have time. You still have time to have a relationship with the Lord, and you still have time for Him to use you. The Word says that the harvest is plentiful, but the workers are few (Matthew 9:35-38). He is and has been waiting on you. He loves you so much and wants your attention. He wants to show you how much He loves you. I promise you if He can love me, forgive me, and give me peace, He can definitely give it to you. He is not a respecter of persons (Romans 2:11–16). He may orchestrate events differently, but He loves us all the same. His love is everlasting, but His wrath is real, and His word will not bend or change. We can't live as lukewarm Christians (Revelations 3:16) and expect the will and peace of God to flow freely. As a matter of fact, the Lord hates lukewarm Christians, and this same scripture says that He will "spew you out of His mouth." He says it's better to be either cold or hot.

FALLING IN LOVE WITH JESUS

I think that most of us started out with a religious relationship with Christ (if there is such a thing). What I mean is that we went through a taught ritual with Christ. This is what I call religion. We went through the motions of doing what we believed God wanted us to do, only to find out later, for most of us much later, that this was not fulfilling and definitely not sustainable. It's not sustainable because that is not what the Lord ordained or wants from us. He wants a true relationship. I have found that it is very difficult to have a true relationship with Christ without falling in love with Him. I am sure that everyone's journey is different as far as a true relationship. Some people read about Jesus and learn of His goodness, and fall in love with Him from the start. I would venture to say that this is a small group of people. Most, as was I, was drawn to His grace, mercy, and how He intervened in my life when I was helpless and had nowhere to turn.

When I was praising God this morning, I was drawn back to the many times that I was at my lowest, even almost near death, and He came through for me. I don't know if this is the total reason that I fell in love with Jesus. I believe for me, it was unconditional love that I have never known. I look back over my life, and I see all of the wrong turns that I have taken and all of the times I have put myself, others, and things before Him. And, He still loved me and accepted me when I called out to Him. This type of love, as we have talked about earlier, is difficult to embrace because it is scarce or nonexistent in this world. Once I truly accepted the Lord's unconditional love and learned that I am worthy of it through Him, that is when I fell in love with Him. During this time, I totally surrendered to Him. I wish it hadn't taken me the journey that I went on to get to this place, but I am equally thankful that I am at this place, and the Lord gave me the grace and mercy to live until I truly embraced Him.

As I ponder over all that is taking place in this world today, I can see the escalation of the spiritual things happening in this world. What I mean is that I can almost tangibly feel the warfare going on in the spiritual realm. Even those who don't know Christ will say things like, "I don't know what's going on in this world." What's even sadder is the fact that those that confess Christ are going through their lives, watching this warfare and ignoring it or not seeing it at all. I am not sure which state is worse. I will go even further and say that those that confess Christ and do see the spiritual warfare going on, and do nothing, are a mystery to me. Some may say, "What am I to do?" Lend yourself to be used by God. Don't write off those that don't know Him. We cannot sit in our bubble and just wait for Jesus to come back or take us to Him and watch those around us go to hell. We cannot do this. I try daily to ask the Lord, "How can You use me on this day?" Then, as I go throughout my day, I expect to encounter an opportunity to be used. It may be someone that He puts in my path that needs a kind word. It may be someone who is hopeless and needs to hear of Christ's love. The list goes on and on. Some days, it's just rendering a smile to someone who may look down. The one thing we cannot do is be afraid.

As I read the Word, I don't see this world getting any better but worse. The Word says that until we repent and turn from our wicked ways, He will not heal our land (2 Chronicles 7:14). I don't know about you, but I don't see our land repenting. I see us going into deeper and deeper sin. It is all around us, and we want nothing to do with God and His principles. Remember, God's Word never changes, whether it's 1923 or 2023. Until we ask the Lord to forgive our disobedience and turn from our ways and invite Him back into all of the places we have pushed Him out of, we will not see a change. On the contrary, we will see further destruction.

So, what is the answer for us individually? There are several. First, be ready, always. Make sure you forgive those whom you hold grudges against, no matter how grievous the offense is. This includes all of the offenses that you are justified to hold on to. The Lord doesn't give us justification not to forgive. He clearly states that if we do not forgive, we won't be forgiven (Matthew 6:14-15). I believe that this is absolute in regard to our relationship with Christ. Let me say this, and I know this to be true. There is no offense, including rape, murder, and so on, that God does not require us to forgive. There is not a sin on this earth that our Father in heaven will not forgive, and He requires the same for us. Again, as we have spoken of earlier, you may not feel the manifestation of this obedience of forgiveness right away, but it is imperative for your right standing with the Lord to be able to go to Him freely. I will promise you that at some point after you have forgiven someone, you will feel the manifestation of it. I will go on to say that sometimes unforgiveness can pop back up in your mind or spirit, and you have to keep forgiving that person. My husband cheating on me many years ago doesn't really bother me anymore, but there are some times that he will say or do something, and my mind and feelings will conjure back up what he did. I have to remind myself that I have forgiven him and no longer hold him accountable. Remember that our forgiveness for that person is us being obedient. That person still needs to seek forgiveness from Christ, and if they do not, they will have to deal with the consequences.

Let me say that again, our forgiveness towards someone is our obedience to Christ. That person still must go to Christ and seek forgiveness for their right standing with Christ. We get to a place where we begin seeing people who have hurt us, especially intentionally, as God sees them. They are broken in areas that we often cannot see. Therefore, they are hurting us out of their hurt. I have often prayed for the Lord to let me see someone as He sees them. I did not say your feelings would line up always, but if you pray the prayer with sincerity for God to move, He will change your heart toward that person. You may want to hold on to the hatred. I have realized in the past that when we hold on to hatred and pain, we feel like we are winning in a sense. We feel, if we forgive that person, we are letting them off the hook. We must overcome those feelings and ignore them. This again goes back to our feelings versus our faith and obedience. When the Lord tells us we must do something, we just have to do it no matter what we feel. As they say, "Fake it until you feel it." I can assure you that doing this will change your heart and make it more like His.

After making sure we are ready, we are in the right standing with Christ, and we have forgiven, we must surrender. This is huge because we cannot be used by the Lord without surrendering our will for His will. This is truly the essence of this book and of our entire journey with Christ, *His will, not mine.* This is single-handedly the number one obstacle in us living for Christ and serving Him at the ultimate level. If I am being totally transparent, and I want to be, I struggle with this daily. I have often held back parts of myself from God for fear that He might take too much or ask for something that I am not willing to do. Okay, everyone, let's keep it real. We all know that if God showed us even half of the things that He would allow or the things He would ask us to do, we would crawl up under our bed and never come out. I'm so glad He doesn't give us a warning.

Surrendering all to God, I believe, is a process, but one that yields us to climb to higher heights in hearing from God and being used by Him. When we are surrendered, God knows that He can trust us. The single factor that has allowed me to surrender as much as I have is the fact that I know the Lord has what's best for me, no matter what. Even unto death, I trust Him. That is a very hard place to get to, and it is a daily surrender. I have even surrendered my children, which is even harder than surrendering myself.

The places I struggle with are selfish ambitions. Things that I want that God may want to change in my life. This is why I try to remember to pray for God to change my heart to His. This morning I asked God to teach me how to love like He does, teach me to surrender, teach me to put others before myself, and teach me to have His mind and seek things that He wants me to. Why? Because in myself, I don't know how. The issue that many have is that we are trying to do things in our strength. We have very limited strength or control. God called us to be many things, but He never asked us to do it in our strength. He wants us to come to Him to do His will. He wants us to come to Him for everything.

THE LORD NEEDS WARRIORS, NOT WHINERS

I believe it has been established and believed by all that this world and its securities are becoming scarce. The United States as a whole has turned away from the very foundation that it was built on: God. The lack of morals and the acceptance of them, even by Christians, is disappointing and disheartening, to say the least. I definitely do not profess to be a Bible scholar, but from what I do know of the Bible and the depiction of what we will go through prior to the second coming of Christ, we are right on schedule. Again, I am not here to spread doom and gloom because those of us in Christ know how the story ends and who has already won in the end. Our eternity is secured. I don't believe that we, followers of Christ, should just sit back and wait for Jesus to return. As a matter of fact, if we do this, I don't feel we can have total peace because that is not God's purpose for us. We are here to spread the Good News and allow the Lord to use us to save the lost.

In saying all of this, we who are here now must get engaged for the kingdom, and in doing this, we will go against the grain, and we will suffer for Christ. What do I mean by suffering? Right now, the Lord needs warriors, not whiners. He needs Christians who are not going to focus on the things of this world, disregarding His kingdom. I have seen in my own life and walk with Christ that I can allow the enemy to side-track me with the things of this world. I am not talking about sin but about being distracted by things that we believe are good things and not checking with the Lord about what He wants us to do. Let me give you a couple of examples from my life.

Though I have been very successful in my sales career, I was constantly trying to get more sales and more money. While I was raising my children, I focused on nothing else but them. If the enemy can throw any obstacle in front of us to focus on, then he can get us to get focused on that and not on the Lord's purpose. These can be small obstacles but constant throughout our life. As I spoke about earlier, humans are all about comfortability. We will do and buy anything that makes life easier for us. I have several very wealthy friends who are amazing people, but they are comfortable in their life. As long as they go to church, volunteer once in a while, and give to the needy, they believe they are doing their duty for the Lord. None of this takes them out of their comfort zone. Am I saying there is anything wrong with these things? Absolutely not, but I believe that the days that we are living in are going to take Christians willing to step out of their comfort zone, seek the Lord and His will, and do it no matter what the cost. I am not there now, but I am praying that the Lord will show me how to be in this place.

Jesus paid too high of a price for people to live their entire life, not knowing that they would spend eternity in hell. If you say that this is not your concern, you might ask yourself, "Do I truly have the mind of Christ, and am I trying to please Him?" I say that because that is the Lord's number one goal: to get His children back. Remember, He said He would leave the ninety-nine that He already has to reach the one that He lost parable in Matthew 18:2. That means that we are going to have to stand up for righteousness. We cannot continue living by the world's standards because we want to fit in or be accepted. I can promise you the time is going to come when you have to go against the grind and be ridiculed, and some will and already are being martyred. I know this sounds deep and difficult. Well, it is deep, and it is difficult in our own strength, but in His strength, we can do it. Let us all think about where we are in our relationship with Christ. Are we seeking Him daily to get His direction, or are we fitting Him into our schedule?

THE FINAL CHAPTER

In this short book, I have tried my best to yield myself to write what God would have me write. As I began writing, I knew that this book was meant to be simple. I guess authors would call it an "easy read." I pray that, in some way, I have displayed truths that I have learned that will truly glorify Him. The journey through life with the Lord is not difficult. We make it difficult when we try and figure out His next move or want to always have things our way, or just don't want to let go of the things of this world that keep us trapped.

One thing is for sure. Jesus is coming back. Either we will hear the trumpet sound, or you will be brought to Him through death on this earth. Either way, we will all stand before God and give an account for our life. I know that sounds scary, but it really isn't if you can stand before Him, who washed off all of your sins through His Son, who paid the ultimate price. Now, if you have to stand before God on your own without the blood of Christ, who paid for all of our sins, you are doomed, and I mean that literally. The Bible says that you will spend the rest of your life in hell (2 Thessalonians 1:8-9). Understand the Lord wants no one to go to hell. Hell was intended for the devil and his angels, not for us (Matthew 25:41). As I have spoken of earlier, I do not have all of the answers. I don't believe anyone here on earth does, but there are many truths that God makes known to all of us (the saved and unsaved), and one truth is that there is only one way to heaven and the Father, and that is through His Son, Jesus Christ (John 14:6). Our heavenly Father made a way for us to live with Him through all eternity even after we fell and were on our way to hell. My friends, there is no other way. There are many controversies in the Bible, but this is not one of them. Some may ask, "Once saved, always saved?" "What is the age of accountability?" "Does Jesus take the dead in Christ first or last?" And so many other debatable questions. None of these delete salvation or the way to salvation.

I ask you today to sit down and look inside your heart. As yourself, if you die today, do you truly believe that you will go to heaven? Remember, no one will go to heaven because of their sins. Our sins have been atoned for on the cross with Jesus. We will only go to hell, and not heaven, if we haven't accepted Christ, who gets rid of our sins. Now, ask yourself, though you have accepted Christ, are you living for Him? I am going to interject and say this. I can't judge who is going to heaven or hell. The Bible says He judges the inside of a man, not the outside (1 Samuel 16:7). I, nor anyone else, know the true state of your heart, but God clearly does. He knows if you truly accepted and loved Him or if you just signed your name on a church role. That's why I ask you to seek your heart and ask the Lord to judge your heart now and not when it's too late. We all, especially young people, believe we have so much time. I don't know about you, but I see more young people dying now than ever. Tomorrow not being promised is not a cliché, and there are no second chances.

If, by chance, you are reading this book, and you have never given your life to Christ, please do so now by asking Him into your heart. Ask Him to give you a new focus and direction in life, His direction. I am not saying that you will wake up tomorrow and all of your problems will be gone, but I will tell you that He will walk with you through this journey called life. He will make it easier to endure because you will be enduring with His strength. You will have someone to cry out to for comfort, and you will be someone that He can use to bring others into the kingdom of God and forego an eternal life of torment.

If you are reading this book and you don't believe in heaven or hell, I pray for you right now in the name of Jesus. I ask that the Lord place people, places, and situations in your path that will make His existence evident to you. You don't need to have all of the answers to accept Christ. Even after you accept Him, you won't have all of the answers, but you will have joy and peace greater than you have ever known. You may say you know people that are Christians and don't have joy and peace. We all do. Do you know why? Because they have not yielded themselves and their life to Christ. They have only acknowledged their belief, which the Bible says, "Even the devil and his demons believes in Jesus and trembles" (James 2:19).

The Lord says that "if we seek Him, we will find Him" (Jeremiah 29:13). Seeking Him is not difficult. You just pray and talk to God and acknowledge that you need Him and that you want Him in your life. Tell Him that you acknowledge all of your past mistakes and sins and that you want Him to help you to live a better life in Him. I know I have said it several times, but you will still make mistakes and fall sometimes. When you do, go to the Lord immediately and confess your sin, and He will be there to forgive you, comfort you, and strengthen you. The devil will surely come and remind you of your sins and the things in your past. He still does it to me. That is a trick to get you not to follow Christ. If the enemy can make you feel that you are not worthy and you don't have the strength to live a Christian life, he can stop you from moving forward. No, you are not worthy, and you do not have the strength to live a Christian life, but God does through His Son. If I tell you the sins that are in my past and the mistakes that I would never speak about, it will blow your mind. Some sins I would never, ever speak about. Jesus has covered those sins, so when they come up in my mind, I remind myself and Satan that those sins are in the past, forgiven and covered by the blood of Jesus. Also, remind Satan that his sins are not forgiven and that he will spend eternity in hell. Do not be afraid of the enemy, and do not let him bully you in your mind. Jesus paid a dear price for your salvation. It was not an easy price to pay. Walk in your inheritance. It doesn't matter what your mind or your feelings tell you; you are forgiven, and you belong to Christ.

I love you, my sisters and brothers, and I am so excited about our journeys here and, more excitedly, after here in heaven. I will be praying for you, and all I ask is that you pray for me. Stay strong during these last days. Stand on the truth that God has given you. Do not get weary, and stay in prayer so that you can stay strengthened.

We are in the middle of a spiritual battle unlike no other. The enemy is trying to stop us from reaching our destinies in Christ, and he is also trying to take our children. Have a boldness for Christ. He was bold when He suffered on that cross for us. I pray that I have said what the Lord wanted me to say and that this book will advance the kingdom, in Jesus' name.

ABOUT THE AUTHOR

Gina is a first-time author who wanted to share many of the lessons that she has learned through mistakes, trials, and tragedies, which have given her a better understanding of the Lord, His will, and His love for us. Her main purpose of this book is for someone to come out of just knowing *of* the Lord by truly knowing who He is and how He wants so much to have a relationship with us. Gina wants anyone reading this book to know that it is not too late to change courses and understand the Lord. No matter the mistakes or shortcomings, Jesus is waiting for us with open arms. In these last days, we must be diligent in not only having a relationship with Christ but putting ourselves in a position to be used by Him to spread the Good News of His love.

So, now that we have surrendered, this is where the fun begins. Those that say living for Christ is boring haven't surrendered to Christ. To watch the way God moves in His might and power is amazing. To watch Him intervene in situations in your life and others is absolutely mind-blowing, and it never gets old. When you wake up every day surrounded by God's peace, it is refreshing.

Printed in the USA
CPSIA information can be obtained
at www.ICGtesting.com
LVHW020701240923
758983LV00002B/11